A Light Shining in a Dark Place

Angela K. Durden

This publication is based on the life and experiences of the author and is considered a memoir.
© 2022 Angela K. Durden All rights reserved.
angeladurden-books.com

ISBN: 978-1-950729-14-2

This publication may not be reproduced, stored in a retrieval system, or transmitted in whole or in part, in any form or by any means, electronic, mechanical, photocopying, recording, or otherwise, without the prior written permission of Angela K. Durden. For permissions, write:

Blue Room Books
blueroombooks@outlook.com
Subject Line: Permissions for Light in Dark Place

Short quotations may be used by newspapers, magazines, and other publications, and online blogs as part of reviews, articles, or reports, but must attribute author and book title.

Cover design and interior layout: Angela K. Durden
Editor: Tom Whitfield

ANGELA K. DURDEN

ONE WOMAN'S
QUEST TO FEEL
LOVE FROM HER
HEAVENLY FATHER

a light shining in a dark place

THE TWINKLE CONTINUES

Just Between Us

I'm writing this preface after I wrote a lot of the book. A book that is heavy and deep and confusing. The thoughts I had were these:

Where are the jokes?
Where's the humor?
Why can't I laugh at myself?
Why is everything so serious?

I'm a funny person. People tell me I'm a real comedienne and that I make a party more fun. People also tell me that my face makes all kinds of expressions that are amazingly diverse. To them I say the following: My face is made for comedy, I just wish it wasn't. Yes! They laugh at that, too, because there it is: That face of mine coming up with some sort of expression that isn't at all what I think it is.

So, why can't I be funny in this book? Why can't I joke about abuse and introspection? Should I go back through the book and see where I should make a joke? I don't know. If you read one, then I hope it makes you laugh.

The Bible says in Proverbs 14:13 that even in laughter the heart may be in pain and the end of that jolly episode is heavy sadness. Well, geez, what I'm writing is already heavy. Why do I want to make it heavier with an ill-fitting joke?

But mostly I don't believe I can joke about — treat lightheartedly — these subjects because, for me, doing that would be to disrespect the victims of abuse and the long-term emotional, psychological, physical, and spiritual fallout they must deal with.

Not only does the victim deal with those things, their family and children and friends do, too. Which brings up a whole other subject: Should one tippy-toe around such victims if to tippy-toe means one must squash that which is normal human relations? I believe yes, only not always. Just as a person with a broken leg must have help and other aids to get around, once that break heals why would we still be lifting them in and out of a wheelchair? Why would this person with the healed leg still carry and use crutches? Makes no sense.

Isn't it up to the victims to recognize they are the ones who have been taken out of the good human relationship spectrum and to find their way back?

I believe it is. In my entire life, I never once thought of myself as a victim. I thought of myself as the person who would find a way to deal with wherever I was. Yet, that very belief about myself was not entirely correct. I was a victim. I was a young child at the mercy of adults. That I had the inclination to find a way to stop that abuse did not mean I was not a victim.

Part of my restoration to normal human thought processes was to recognize I had been a victim, was hurt, and needed healing. I'll cover this deeper in **Courage and Cowardice and Wisdom.**

Put it this way: If I broke my leg and did not get it set so it could heal, the leg would make me a cripple and could lead to infection and other issues. Ignoring psychological, emotional, and spiritual breaks as if they did not exist caused me, for one example, to pick a husband who was exactly like my mother and, for the second example, allowed me to remain stationary in personal growth for far, far too long.

When finally I recognized that I *must* grow, I had a horrible thought: My marriage will end. So, being the can-do person I am, I believed I could stop even that from happening. I was wrong. That was not a decision I made alone; surprise-surprise, I found my husband didn't want to be married to the healed me.

As he said just before I moved out: "Look, when I married you I just wanted to have a quiet wife who would do what I told her. Who would cook, do laundry, clean the house, take care of the kids, help with my parents, and f**k me." (His words.)

The heck of it was, I did all that and more. Yes, I was even quiet — until I couldn't be and had to stand up for myself. Yet my husband was never happy. Just like Mother. I get into this more in the **Pretzeling** chapter. My introspection has been a painful journey whose end has not yet been reached. Maybe that journey will only end when I die, so dead is not something I am afraid of being.

Also note that this book is being written from the perspective of a Christian woman. Scriptures are cited and quoted. It is not my intention to get "doctrinal" or trash or uplift any particular religion. The journey is mostly spiritual but with psychological and emotional benefits as well. I ask neither that you agree or disagree with what I write: I care not which. All I can hope is that what I write will simply give you food for thought on your journey and help clarify the path you take.

That I May Learn

I'm running, running, running, frantically running through a cityscape that is an amalgamation of several cities but calling itself Los Angeles. Dodging water that was everywhere. Some falling from the sky, some from water fountains intent on spewing more wildly when I passed. Carrying a newspaper I want to read but holding up to keep hair dry.

Slogging wet-footed through winding basement areas filled with little nooks and crannies featuring trendy restaurants serving vile garbage artfully arranged. Slipping on wet grass. Sinking to my knees in unseen holes in lawns and holding the newspaper up high and out of the holes to keep some part of it readable.

I'm in a hurry to get to the stadium to meet Mother and siblings but I'm finding it impossible to get there because everything reroutes me away from it. I'm getting desperate, desperate I tell ya! Finally, hope. I see the stadium. Huge. Like something out of the Jetsons but in real life. Cars whiz by throwing water up from a busy thoroughfare that somehow must be crossed, but my feet won't move and I get more soaked. I become more desperate. I will be too-too late.

More obstacles thrown in my path slowing me, attempting to knock me down, kill me! Mother and siblings will die if I don't get to them.

I cry out, "Oh, God, help me."

I do not understand. Other people are crossing the street, but my feet are planted firmly. I stare from the stadium to my feet to the paper and back to the stadium as huge bells atop it begin to chime most beautifully, one after another.

But the bells turn out to be text messages from my bank. A deposit has been made. Only dreaming, I wake as if drugged, upset, but do not know the reason.

Quickly dressing so as to get to my social media page before I forget, I tell this most hilarious dream because I am a writer who likes to give friends and fans something entertaining to read.

I had not thought to look for a meaning deeper than my normal explanation for my vibrant and complicated dreams: Ah, she's a

A Light Shining in a Dark Place — 11

creative and creatives dream creatively. But after several folks attempted to interpret it, and realizing their explanations made me bow up in frustration and, remembering how upset I was upon waking from it, I wondered if the dream was representing something in my life to which attention was badly needed.

One comment on the post caused a dawning, and a scripture came to mind. Ecclesiastes 3:7: There is *"…a time to keep quiet and a time to speak…"*

I had worked so hard, sometimes furiously so, to find God's love through a deep understanding of the Bible that His love was completely missed. He knew it and told me what to do, which was to hush, keep quiet, and wait. And so on this morning of sharing some of my dream on social media and seeing a comment, that scripture was remembered. The Bible book, written by King Solomon, comprised 12 chapters and 222 verses. My eye fell upon verses 16 and 17 of chapter three:

> *"And I have further seen under the sun the place of justice where there was wickedness and the place of righteousness where wickedness was. I myself have said in my heart: 'The true God will judge both the righteous one and the wicked one, for there*

is a time for every affair and concerning every work there.'"

Thus my dream above had the same message as this Bible chapter: The want for certain justice may be mine, but the power to make it happen is not. Therefore, on what do I want to spend my time? Verse 22:

"And I have seen that there is nothing better than that man should rejoice in his works, for that is his portion; because who will bring him in to look on what is going to be after him?"

In other words, my focus should be on the now, as Jesus' brother said in James 4:14-16:

"…whereas you do not know what your life will be tomorrow. For you are a mist appearing for a little while and then disappearing. Instead, you ought to say: 'If Jehovah wills, we shall live and also do this or that.' But now you take pride in your self-assuming brags. All such taking of pride is wicked."

Stop living in the past. Stop worrying about the future. And work on that big ol' ego that was so carefully cultivated by Satan during my abuse-filled childhood. And what an ego it was. Only *I* could save the family from the evil of my stepfather. Only…I couldn't. Justice was not mine to serve and thus the frustration of the dream.

And so yet again upon reading Ecclesiastes 3 on that dream-filled morning, unlike on previous partial readings, I began to feel a glimmer of delight in God's love. His words reminded me of my place. My place was not to exalt myself, but to serve Him as best I could where I stood and make myself available for His will, whether or not I knew what that was.

So I stand. I stand in the place my Heavenly Father has pushed me to be and I wonder when I will learn to stop kicking against the goads. But, as Psalm 119:71 says:

> *"It is good for me that I have been afflicted,*
> *In order that I may learn your regulations."*

A few friends and acquaintances from my "church-going" days have alternately accused me of turning my back on my Heavenly Father as if I no longer believe He exists. Some spread rumors that I left God because I wanted to have fun by practicing evil, or as others might say, "She wanted to go wild."

Well, I didn't leave God nor go wild, but felt my reputation was being besmirched. So, like righteous Prince Hezekiah, I begged God. Beset with major problems in his own family [father was evil King Ahaz] and in the two-tribe nation [most Jews were unfaithful and enemy nations were trying to take over], the future King of Judah said in Psalm 199:176:

> *"I have wandered like a lost sheep. O look for your servant, For I have not forgotten your own commandments."*

And yet, Hezekiah was not lost. He only looked and felt like he was. We know he wasn't lost because his Heavenly Father had His eye upon him; He knew where the young man was and had already set his course.

This has been my same experience. I thought I was lost. Certainly, felt as if I was. But Daddy had his eye upon me and was guiding my steps. So, are we really lost if someone knows where we are?

A Light Shining in a Dark Place — 15

Like a lot of people, I don't like uncertainty, want to know where I'm going and why, how long it will take to get there, and where *there* is. "Are we there yet, Daddy? Are we there yet?"

Our Heavenly Father must often feel like that parent. His patience is not short, but that does not mean we will always understand it.

Naturally, the next thing to ask will be, "Exactly *how* is God using *you*?"

In this I am not answering the reader for one very good reason: I can look back and see a few random places *where* He's placed me. Sometimes I can see *what* I did. But I have not always learned the *why* of it or *how* it fit into any big plan. Who can know the mind of God and how He will make anything happen?

Let me explain a bit further. My ex-husband and his father were brilliant when it came to building, fabricating, repairing, etc. Both had been told many times "That can't be done!" only to turn around and do it. One of their projects even got them in the newspaper it was so wonderful. I learned a lot from both of these men during the years I was married. They found ways to make something happen that I had not thought of. Seeing the parts and the whole came as naturally to them as breathing.

But not for me.

Even as I watched. Even as it made perfect sense right that minute. Even as I could hammer with the best of them. Even with all that, I could not of and by myself build a house. I couldn't even build a simple wall. The details were beyond my ability to figure out.

For instance, they would be drilling holes that, to me, seemed willy-nilly, without rhyme or reason. But when the whole was put together, why, I could see the holes were for wires to run through according to where outlets and switches would be placed.

What? Wires run through the walls?

Of course they do, but I did not think of that. A switch just existed and worked! Boom. Done. Cars only ran because of gas. Lights only worked because of switches. Eggs came from the grocery store…just kidding about this one. But they saw the whole house and its parts at the same time.

In the same manner, our Heavenly Father sees the whole and the parts of His purpose and plans at the same time. He has a purpose and that purpose remains constant. But the plans to make that purpose come to fruition can change.

If I cannot understand a simple thing like a wall, then how can I ever understand the mind of God? It is impossible, therefore I will not attempt to explain the *why* of His attention on me. I can only report that the attention exists, what has happened with it, my response to it, and how it's turning out for me. There will be some confusion and gaps in these writings as there is in all of life.

I do not claim to be a prophet nor to have all the answers. I write only to figure out for myself about myself so my relationship with my Heavenly Father can grow. This is between me and God. As TV commercials say in the fine print: Your experience may differ.

Angela K. Durden

---

2 Corinthians 12:7, the Apostle Paul:

"Therefore, that I might not feel overly exalted, there was given me a thorn in the flesh, an angel of Satan, to keep slapping me, that I might not be overly exalted."

Notes to help the reader understand what follows:

To honor the privacy of my siblings and mother who wish not to be in the public eye, but so you will know the birth order of my younger siblings (I am the oldest of five) I use the following:

Devil = When discussing my stepfather

Mother = Mother

Little Sister = Second-born sibling

Baby Brother = Third-born sibling

Little Baby Brother = Fourth-born sibling

Baby Baby Brother = Fifth-born sibling (born when I was 17 and was three when his father died, so he did not get the abuse from his father that the other siblings did).

To get a fuller picture of my journey or to shed light when you wonder about certain examples in these pages, please read *This Little Light of Mine: Twinkle Revisited*.

2008: Open Letter to God

Dear God,

For all I know about you, I know nothing. You are a complicated guy. I don't know why that surprises me. I am complicated and supposedly you are my father so maybe the nut didn't fall far from the tree. Which is why the more I learn about you the more I believe you do understand my mind …I have prayed to you in many ways. You have ignored me — and rightly so, for some of those prayers are just weird.

The majority of my stress is in trying to figure out how not to hurt people in the congregation, in the family, in the world.

I am mad at you, too. I know you have more to worry about than me, but it would be nice to feel special and know for sure that specialness was real and not a wish or figment of my imagination. Yet, it seems that somehow it is my responsibility to prove Satan wrong and you right — at my expense.

You have no problem making your emotional needs known and being justified in so doing, but boy! let me demand and all of a sudden I am selfish and wrong because I'm supposed to give of myself and not think too much of myself? It is not fair. I want a divorce. You know my needs and desires. Please…

Just make it happen!

Sincerely, Angela

Ego and Shelter

A song by Robert Clark "Bob" Seger recounts the slow passing of years and of being alone yet surrounded by strangers and searching for shelter *Against the Wind*.

I found myself in the same position when divorcing after 32 years of marriage. My book *Twinkle — a memoir* [out of print], written to help me make sense of where I was, did not include many vignettes originally written because they were alike emotionally, psychologically, or spiritually to others I'd written. Therefore, I chose only those stories that best defined my life's path.

In these I was looking for evidence of God's love and so chose to write of the events that included demonstrable proof that God — even if I had questioned Him or His existence — had been or was there and thus would always be in my future.

Therefore, very focused on that, I did not see that the emotional journey I had taken to the top of my little "Blue Ridge foothill" was for others the equivalent of climbing Mount Kilimanjaro while feeling rumblings underfoot and wondering if the long-dormant volcanic peaks were going to blow. To top it all off, not a single clue was provided to readers in order for them to prepare for that journey. I started suddenly, unaware of the hazards to others, fully expecting folks to casually follow along to a good ending they could not have foreseen.

Gut punches came too fast for those unused to gut punches.

Another surprise kept coming my way, too. People said, "Wow. That was powerful. When are you going to write your follow-up and tell us about the rest of it?" My answer was always the same. "The rest of it? Hmmm…not sure about that."

Sorry to say, I was not yet at that point where I could write a full memoir about the journey because it was still unclear. Instead, I updated the original memoir to correct those gaps mentioned above, included a foreword and afterword, changed the title, and released it in 2020, five years after the original had been released, entitling it *This Little Light of Mine: Twinkle Revisited*.

However, I had already started writing my thoughts down about the journey I was on after writing the memoir. Updating it gave me more time to ponder in a more focused fashion. Yes, things were becoming clearer.

Those who read my memoir noted I had a deep longing for a mother who loved me. To this day, that has not happened with Mother…and it never will. I cannot stand the story of Don Quixote, he being a dreamer wishing for and chasing after that which was unattainable. What a waste of time, said my practical self. But there I was, a Don Quixote tilting after the windmill called my mother.

But another surprise was in store. It is detailed in the section entitled **Healing and Truth**. It let me know my Heavenly Father is still watching because He sent something that was so good I could not have foreseen it.

Friedrich Nietzsche said, "That which does not kill us, makes us stronger." Ol' Friedrich sure did love his all-or-nothing statements. I hate all-or-nothing statements because, while there is a nugget of truth in each, they are usually factually incorrect in the bigger context — the one that matters.

The fact of the matter is "that which does not kill us" can keep one weak, can foster the comfort of the victim mentality, can make one fail to see Truth and/or act on behalf of Good.

There can be no sacrifice unless stakes are high. Was I willing to take actions that sacrificed something about myself that I held dear but was bad for me? If so, what would those be?

For one thing, my reputation. I got hung up on that and imbued it with a power over my life that kept me from moving forward.

Against all the destructive messaging I got growing up and in my marriage, messaging that wanted me to believe I was bad, I did not feel I was a bad person. Every now and then came positive messaging that supported my belief that I was a good girl, a good wife, a good mother.

Which would I believe: The lies or the truths? But which were lies? Which were truths? One destroyed my reputation and the other gave me a good reputation within my own mind. Was I fooling myself when believing good about myself and attempting to reject the negative? Or was I truly the bad person Mother and her husband and my husband said I was?

My good reputation was a big deal because it was all I ever had that was mine and I very much wanted to hold on to it. I found out as an adult that even God is jealous of and defends His reputation against slander and other character assassinations. (Exodus 34:14; Numbers 11:29; Deuteronomy 32:16, 21; 1 Kings 14:22; Psalm 78:58; 1 Corinthians 10:22; 2 Corinthians 11:2) But I didn't know that as a child. All I knew was that to defend my reputation meant not offering myself up as a sacrificial lamb, yet defending myself meant letting Mother and siblings be hurt.

So my definition of "good girl" became limited on two fronts. One: By not being like Mother. And two: Ignoring God's hand in a matter because I listened to others when they said that God couldn't possibly mean *that*, whatever *that* was to them.

Some say they believe God is not limited, but they are mistaken because God deals with each human where their specific limits are. Which means God Himself lives with self-imposed limits. So, when I finally understood that God did mean exactly what He wanted me to understand, that allowed me to take action. Action that for most people might not work, and for which I have been and continue to be condemned. **(See song lyrics in the back entitled** *God Is Not A Race***.)** But God met me where I was, giving what was needed in order to know Him best that I may be of best service to Him.

Do I believe? Yes, I do. More so than ever do I see His expansive hand…and I do not mean in a "pie in the sky" kind of way. One can say that when Almighty God goes against popular opinion, He himself is putting His reputation on the line. That is a sacrifice He made that I will not squander no matter who disagrees or does not understand.

I have stresses, true, but my life is turning out well. There are fewer barriers between me and my Heavenly Father now. Trust of Him has grown. I more quickly accept His guidance and see the good things He sends my way. When things don't go as planned, I fret much less and not nearly as long.

Life and business on hold while I looked after my Aunt Pearl until her death **(See Healing and Truth)**, here I am again, exploring my continuing journey. To do that, I reread *Twinkle*. Besides what I mentioned in the introduction, my second response was this: Wow. Who is this person? Have I changed? And, dare I say it, improved? Well, let's just stick with change and assume that the change is for the better, okay? Must stay positive.

Rereading my memoir, I made notes on the inside back cover of topics needing exploring.

But how to organize these so that the telling was logical and not meandering hokum? I decided to get basic to that which is true for all humans.

There are three things that affect every person on the earth at all times: Nature. Nurture. Free Will. What are the effects of each?

Nature is our inherited traits. Passed along to us through DNA. Over which we exert little to no control. In this instance I speak not only of the physical but of the character, personality, temperament, disposition, spirit, and humor of a person. Mother used to always ask, "Who are you? Where did you come from?" because my character, personality, temperament, disposition, spirit, and humor were so unlike her, her other children, or her mother and that side of the family. Apparently, other than having a physical relationship, she didn't know my father very well or she would not have asked such questions.

Nurture is that which we receive from others and, in a bigger sense, eventually learn to do for and to ourselves — good or bad, love or abuse. Nature will always direct how Nurture is processed, thus making psychologists' and psychiatrists' jobs harder since one rule cannot apply to all equally.

But the foundation for the other two is **Free Will**. It can modify those so that even if Nature wants us to do X and Nurture says X is a good thing, Free Will can say, "Hey, Nature! Yo, Nurture! Listen up. You're both wrong. I forbid you to do that."

Or Free Will and Nurture want us to do Y but Nature recoils from Y. Or...well, you get the drift. Only we can decide which is strongest and will have the most say in any given situation. Which is why our Heavenly Father is so patient with us. It is only through His undeserved kindness that we have a chance.

Which brings us back to me.

Abuse, especially incest because of the sexual nature of it, often produces in certain children a sense that they are all-powerful. I was that type of child. You see, according to my stepfather, he only did what he did to me because I was so, so very cute and sexy and he just couldn't stay away. Oh, how I tried hard not to be cute and sexy but I didn't know what those things meant so my efforts just didn't work, therefore my mysterious cuteness was ever so exceptionally powerful.

Mother, on the other hand, looked to me from the time I was two-and-a-half to save her because, you see, only I could save her, an adult, from another adult. "Please, Angela, do this for me. I need you to do this" was her plea often "so he won't beat me".

That is heady stuff for any child, but especially for someone with my particular temperament. I have been accused of being a bulldozer. If it needs doing, I get it done. Do not get in my way. I grew up with an inflated though *highly inaccurate* assessment of my power. Yet that inflated assessment did, in point of fact, often save my mother and siblings.

Because adults told me I could, I did.

They were not surprised because, you see, they believed it about me. Still, because my bulldozer temperament also is one of questioning and confirming, major irreconcilable differences abounded, causing much confusion in this little girl's storm-tossed mind. A mind that can only get to the shelter that could only be found in the love of Daddy, my Heavenly Father.

But how to get to that shelter and allow it to protect me? Was I worth protecting? What value did I have in anyone's eyes? Would I be missed if I were gone?

Through the years others have suggested as my theme songs the following:

Angie Baby by Helen Reddy, a story of madness and murder.

Angie by the Rolling Stones, a story of thwarted love and frustration wrought by Angie on poor men who really, really tried.

What a Day for a Daydream by The Lovin' Spoonful, a story of love not found but wow does one have high hopes it will come.

Contradictions galore confused everybody I ran across. In attempting to figure that out, in 2021 I made a partial list of all the things that are the conundrum that is Angela. Some of these have been pointed out to me by others. Some I discovered. In no particular order of importance, they are:

- Empath yet suspicious and wary
- Dyslexic and autistic
- Autodidact polymath
- Creative introvert
- Genius and futile inventor
- Clueless and dangerous
- Sexy hot and frigid bitch
- Performer and entertainer
- Impatient and long-suffering
- Focused and eager
- Insecure and self-confident
- Persistent and daydreamer
- Angry and intense and happy and sad
- Sensitive and self-contained
- Complex and simple

And more categories and adjectives, but why beat this dead horse? All prodding many (including my ex-husband) to say: "Who are you?"

Some of these things I have only just learned about myself; others have only now been accepted after fighting against them. Each has gone a long way in helping me understand how my brain works and why I had so many problems with certain things as far back as I could remember.

But is it shelter I'm looking for? To me, shelter means safety and safety means boring. Of all the things I hate, to be bored is highest on my list. I would rather die than be bored and have sought mightily never to be that. At the same time, I am most comfortable being the new kid on the block, the stranger in the room, the unknown element. These two things — boredom and comfort — often work at cross-purposes to each other.

After awhile, being the stranger in the room with a mind that works like mine simply means I've got new strangers pegged pretty quickly — BORING! (There is nothing new under the sun. Ecclesiastes 1:9) But I also want to be missed and if I'm always the stranger and never go back, then how will I ever know the feeling of being missed?

Even in my religious life, I never felt missed. If I did manage to see someone from a previous congregation, they would always say something about how I was missed because "you sure do cook good" or "you sure knew how to make a party lively" or "you sure were helpful to me when…".

But did they really miss *me*? No. They wanted what I could do for them. To be fair, could I say I really missed them? In fact, my superpower, honed over multiple childhood leavings overnight, never saying goodbye or going back, was this: Only remembering every house, address, and phone number we ever had.

People ceased to be. Poof. Gone.

They mattered not.

I've been practicing on being missed and of missing. Every now and then I feel missed and I feel as if I miss. For instance, I have been in a writing critique group since 2009. I've wanted the group on our downtime! The last time I had felt that missing (of my father not coming to get me) I was nine. The first time I felt that was horrible and vowed never to allow myself to feel that again. Yet here I stood, in the parking lot at the end of my first session in 2009, and wailed, "What am I going to do? I can't wait two months!"

But someone said to me, "You'll be fine. See you in January."

See. You. In. January.

See YOU in JANUARY.

SEE you. SEE you. SEE YOU.

Those words helped me through those most difficult months. That need of being around people who understood the writer in me was bigger than my need for learning to feel the missing. I hated those two off-months.

Remembering that feeling of the first time and now reliving it in the parking lot, I retreated into my typical stand-apart mentality and relegated myself to being the stranger in the room once again. Oh, I said all the right things like "Hey, it's good to see you again", but I wasn't feeling it. Didn't allow myself to.

But a strange thing happened. As Bob Seger sang, the years rolled slowly past. There came a point where, other than the person who started the group, I was the member who'd been there most consistently and the longest. Internally I was still the outsider, the stranger, but I remembered a lot of the people who had come and gone. I even felt myself wondering if they had ever finished their book and where life had taken them.

And you know what? It really was good to see folks again when our breaks were over and we'd get back together. Color me shocked. That

A Light Shining in a Dark Place

was a huge step forward. So I question and compare. Question, validate. Question, accept?

Whew. Acceptance.

That is difficult.

Nevertheless, here I go, still trying to figure me out. But why?

Why not just accept my limitations, live with them, and allow God to surprise me?

First of all, I have, I do, and He does. (Angela plans. God laughs kindly.)

Second, I am a goad kicker. That's why when God was prodding me to leave my husband (a good thing for me), I kept kicking back and saying, "Ah, you don't really mean *that*. You can't really mean *that*. Prove to me you mean *that*. Prove it again because there is no way you can mean *that*."

Four years it took before He finally managed to prove beyond a shadow of a doubt that He meant it and got me to stop kicking back at Him and listen and obey. Why am I like that? Blame it on DNA and such. Still, it wasn't that I didn't want to do what He said. It was that I was so highly focused on a narrow and small set of Big Gotta-Do's that I missed all other acceptable options.

And talk about missing: There is the idea of once again having a husband. I thought I wanted to be married again. Truly I did. Even said as much to a whole crowd of people at a book signing right after the divorce. But now?

I'm no longer liking the idea of marriage, but there will be more on that process in the section entitled **Putting It Together**.

Courage and Cowardice and Wisdom

The Apostle Paul said, "If possible, as far as it depends upon you, be peaceable with all men." (Romans 12:18)

And so I worked at peace awfully hard. But after trying everything to get along and heal wounds with Mother and siblings, those efforts did not work and staying away became the better part of valor. It took courage to stay away from family. My slow reaction to taking a stand had to do with my reputation. What would people think when I don't visit Mother? Yes, the family talked badly about me and inferred much evil or lack of care or whatever it is they wanted to infer. Staying away meant letting those slung stones and flung arrows fly but simply not being where they landed.

Paul said "if possible". He said "as far as it depends upon you".

I did my part but could make no headway with Mother and siblings, and no longer willing to suffer for no good reason, simply did not call or write to them anymore.

Many years ago, early one morning, Little Sister called and asked if I would go with her to a psychologist. I readily agreed. She then said, "Great! The appointment is in an hour." Well, I had a sick kid at home. I couldn't go then and explained to her. She became furious and accused me of not ever caring for her. I explained over and over that I couldn't leave my sick child and asked if it was possible to go the next time she went.

The answer was an emphatic and immediate No. She never forgave me for not going right that minute to solve all her problems. In fact, when I asked about how her sessions were going, she said she quit because it was obvious that I didn't care.

Some years later I began talk therapy with a psychologist. When the doctor asked how long I saw this process lasting, my reply was quick and definitive: Three weeks. My goal? To be a better wife and mother so my husband and children will not be inconvenienced. So, just answer my questions, I told her, and I'll be fine. Her reply was slower but equally definitive: Well, it usually takes as long as it takes. I popped back: Right. It will take three weeks.

A Light Shining in a Dark Place — 37

This bulldozer was wrong!

I was with her for one year. But during that time I proceeded to do something my mother and siblings were not used to…or at least it appeared they were not used to. I spoke of secrets. Secrets kept from each other. Little Baby Brother had been kept in the dark for his protection. I did some really tough things for the rest of the family that they didn't know about. Little Sister and Baby Brother remembered nothing of their childhoods. Mother's memory was…well, we'll talk about that later.

I'm a writer. Thus came the bright idea of writing "open letters". Simply telling them my stories of growing up. Each would get the same letter. All mailed on the same day.

Here's my next surprise: They all talked to each other…or so said Mother because next thing you know a short chastising letter and a phone call came from Mother relaying all the angst stirred up. Everybody was mad at me because, she said, I accused her of being a bad mother.

Now I'm hurt and feel betrayed. I am hurt bad. I had done things no child should be asked to do so that Mother would escape a beating. So, okay. Is that how you want to play? Then it is on, and I fired back with open letter number two wherein I recounted the phone call and letter from Mother who was speaking on their behalf and then proceeded to add to the letter more history and how open dialogue about shared history would be beneficial, blah, blah.

Baby Brother calls and is furious at me for attacking Mother.

Little Baby Brother calls and says it ain't helping so I should stop it.

But did I listen? No! I was in therapy, see, and it was helping with my life. Couldn't they see this was good for them? Boom! Letters three, four, five, six and, if memory serves correctly, seven flew through the USPS like heat-seeking missiles full of healing and love.

Only they weren't. What a self-righteous pricklet I was. In 2019, copies of these letters turned up in my file cabinets. I was particularly dismayed at how clumsy I was in approaching the subject with my family. No wonder they got mad. But then again, they were mad at me even when I didn't bring up anything, *sooo*…

After awhile I realized that Mother and siblings were not going to change and that I had to stand up for myself. Funny thing, though, is that the very husband I divorced (and who himself did not want to transform and would not) is the same one who gave me the ability to see my family clearly. He first gave me permission to tell Little Sister to take a hike. Shortly after we married, I was taking Little Sister around town to pay her bills and get her errands done. She didn't have a vehicle. After an hour of her screaming at me in the car, I put her out on the side of the road and told her to walk home.

Oh Lord, have mercy on me. Hell rained down from Mother and Little Sister about that. While I cried at the drama, putting her out of the car and driving off made me feel a power I had never felt before. I could say no.

I —

Could say —

Was allowed —

Had said —

No.

And lived to tell.

Hard lesson to practice and Husband encouraged me to do it. But when I started saying no to him about his subtle but nonetheless ever-increasing abusive ways… well, don't you know that would not do?

My cowardice, on the other hand, continuously haunts me. Obviously I acted cowardly when I hid in the hallway and watched as the cigarettes were brought out and Mother was being threatened by her husband with being burnt when I was eleven. I did not step in at that time. I kept watch, but hid, not throwing myself between Mother and my stepfather. That night I could not make myself do anything for her. Why? Because I was too worried about myself. That emotional reaction was so strong that for years when I did not "step in" and "rescue" I went through days of beating myself up.

Step in and rescue who, you ask? Well, this is where emotional-reaction training becomes a weakness. It could be something as simple as two strangers sitting in a restaurant having an argument, but I just turn my head.

COWARD!

Yes, that simple. Nothing life-threatening in and of itself. But the emotional reaction was as strong as standing in that hall berating myself for not saving Mother from the threat of being burned. I've had to work so hard to overcome this. As soon as it appears I've done so, up pops another opportunity to scream at myself.

Surprise! You're still a coward!

That internal message, along with one other (You are a slut and only good for one thing!), have been the hardest to overcome. I keep setting myself up to practice having courage. But one does not have courage. One can only act with courage when the time comes.

Speaking up or not is, of and by itself, neither courageous nor cowardly. Doing them at the right time, though — deep breath — takes wisdom. Wisdom I continue to work on having. Prayer is involved. Of course. And being open to receiving in a timely fashion the answers He sends. Definitely.

Without wisdom one can swagger or one can be cowardly. But wisdom pushes cowardice aside, supports courage, and teaches that silence is often the right thing.

I am comforted with the thought in 1 John 3:21, where he says, "Beloved ones, if our hearts do not condemn us, we have freeness of speech toward God; and whatever we ask we receive from Him, because we are observing His commandments and are doing the things that are pleasing in His eyes."

Journal Note, August 8, 2009
Where headship is lacking, subjection cannot exist beneficially.

Sibling Update

Little Baby Brother and I now talk regularly on the phone. We get together and share a meal and have nice visits. We found we have things in common, like singing. Even if he did go astray for a bit, he is still the sweetie pie he always was, wishing and hoping for peace in the family before he dies. He once told me, "Angie, I always thought I was the black sheep of the family. Imagine my surprise to find out the black sheep was you!" If he could only have our mother and siblings in one room at the same time and it be good, fun, and happy, he could die a happy man.

What he doesn't understand, and never will, and what I've come to have peace about, is this: Happy-happy will never materialize. In his heart of hearts he knows it, but he tries to ignore the reality because it makes him sad and he doesn't like to be sad. Recently Mother invited him to the house to have lunch with Little Sister. He called and reported that everybody was on their best behavior and it was a nice visit — even though he tip-toed around subjects he wanted to talk about. In any case, I was happy for him.

A Light Shining in a Dark Place — 43

Yet the last time Little Sister, Baby Baby Brother, Mother, and Little Baby Brother were all in the same room with me — a restaurant — nobody had a good time. A cousin had come to visit me from California. It had been years since she'd seen her aunt, my mother, and she really wanted to see as many relatives on our side as possible while she was here. I recommended she call Mother and make the arrangements and that if Mother didn't want me to be there, I was happy to drive her up and get lost while she visited.

Cousin said that would not happen. Either we all visited together or she wasn't going to see them. Cousin called Mother. Mother was excited. Arrangements were made to meet at a Mexican restaurant in Helen, Georgia. Baby Baby Brother brought his wife and young daughter as well.

There we were. Sitting around the table. Everybody happy to see Cousin and get to know her. Cousin is asking questions and Little Sister pops out with a story. Everybody was laughing and I added some interesting and fun details. Cousin and Little Baby Brother laughed along with me, but Mother, Little Sister, and Baby Baby Brother and his wife all stopped laughing and turned their heads away. Little Sister sniffed self-righteously, frowned in my general direction, "I was not talking to you." The other three nodded in agreement.

Cousin couldn't believe it.

Little Sister then turned to Cousin and began smiling and laughing and telling more stories, but Cousin had a very difficult time from that point on. The meal was tasteless.

After about an hour or so, it was time to adjourn. I said I had brought my camera that had a timer, and a tripod, for a group picture since we were all together with Cousin. After more drama about who would be in the picture, I finally managed to get everybody in one place, set the timer on the camera, clicked the shutter, and went toward the group. Mother said, "You're going to be in the picture, too?" I barely had time to answer yes and set my face in a smile before the shutter clicked.

Cousin was hugged and everybody said goodbye to her. Only Little Baby Brother spoke to me and I was again studiously ignored by the rest. I put my camera and tripod in the car and waited for Cousin. We watched everybody drive away and got in the car. I started shaking and crying. Cousin was furious and had plenty to say on the way back to Atlanta.

As of this writing, that was the last time I saw Mother, Little Sister, and Baby Baby Brother, or my sister-in-law and niece. In 1993,

Baby Brother, who lives in New York state, made it clear he didn't want to hear from me because it was obvious I didn't care about him since I moved out of the house and left him when I was 19. But then around 2001 or so, he was making the Georgia rounds and brought his new wife and his daughter from a previous marriage to see us.

His wife had an opportunity to quietly say to me, "You aren't anything like I expected." Then she smiled. Encouraged, I made another phone call to him just to have a quick how-ya-doing chat and got from him, "Why do you call me?" When I said it was because I loved him and wanted to talk to my brother and keep in contact, he made it clear not to do that anymore.

Around 2016, I got a phone call from Little Baby Brother who wanted to know if we could ride together to New York for the wedding. What wedding? After some discussion it became clear that I had not received an invitation to the wedding of Baby Brother's daughter. Little Baby Brother was furious and said he was going to get me an invitation or find out why I had not gotten one. No amount of begging not to do that would stop him.

A couple of hours later he calls back. Cussing. Furious. He was not going to the blankety-blank wedding since I was not invited. But he asked: Have you been kicked out of the church?

I laughed, said I had not, and wondered why he would ask. He said Baby Brother said I was not invited because he knew for a fact I'd been kicked out because Mother and Little Sister said so.

Little Baby Brother had called Mother who confirmed that yes, Angela had been expelled and since they were good Christians who did not associate with such a bad person who had turned her back on God…

Well, didn't that just bring back memories of living in Red Oak and having Devil excommunicate me from the family when I was thirteen-ish?

I'm telling you all this to say that I cannot report on anything definitive with the family. I'm telling you all this to say that I'm getting depressed just writing it. I'm telling you all this to say nothing will change with them and nothing I do can change how they think about me or treat me.

I'm telling you all this to say that I now better understand the Apostle Paul's advice in Romans 12:18 when he talked of the limits of influence.

Nothing I can do will make them love me, want me, care for me. To try to push myself upon them does not bring peace. They are grownups. They are responsible for their own actions. It is easy to believe them when they say they do not want my company. And I honor their right to say it and no longer try to force myself upon them in the guise of "family healing".

I have finally, thoroughly, accepted my limitations with my family.

As far as it depends upon me....

That is freeing.

Mother

For some years, Mother worked at a popular hotel in a tourist town in the mountains of Georgia. My husband and I wanted to go to that town and so I called Mother to find out if there were any openings on the dates we needed. There were. We arrived and checked in. The next morning her manager said to me, "You must love your mother very much. She is so kind and helpful and sweet."

"*My* mother?"

The manager seemed confused. "Your mother is [Name Here], isn't she?"

I jumped through hoops to explain away that reaction and made a funny joke out of it. The manager laughed with me and all was well. Still, in my entire life I had never had anyone come up to me and say my mother was kind, helpful, and sweet. In fact, nobody ever had an opinion about her one way or the other that was said in my presence. This was a first and my response was truthful from my experience with her. But a public insult was definitely not kind to her and I went out of my

A Light Shining in a Dark Place — 49

way the next couple of days to happily chat at the counter, give her a hug or wave, and "talk her up" to the staff. The effort wore me out.

Fast-forward fifteen years or so. My divorce was over and my granddaughter came to stay with me for a week during the summer. I wanted to take her to that town and spend a couple of days since the last time she'd been there she was barely four. I had heard that Mother no longer worked at the hotel, so I felt safe in calling and not getting her. She answered. Shocked at hearing her voice, I stumbled a bit over my words, but finally got around to checking availability. She tapped at the computer.

"Will this be for one or two?"

"Two."

"Will you want one king-sized bed or two queens?"

"Whatever is available will be fine."

After more clicking around the screen, she then said, "What name will this be booked under?" I gave her mine, along with credit card info, and the room was officially booked. I said thank you. Then she said —

"May I ask: Am I speaking to my daughter?"

"If you are [Her Name Here], then yes, you are speaking to your daughter."

"Ah. I see." And she hung up.

The reader is probably thinking, "Man, that is some kind of weird exchange." And the reader would not be incorrect. But what the reader needs to understand is this: Mother recognized my voice immediately and I knew it. How? Because her voice changed from professional hotelier to the righteously indignant mother I was used to hearing. Therefore, here is the exchange again with added notations in italics:

I had heard that Mother no longer worked at the hotel, so I felt safe in calling and not getting her. *She answered professionally, confidently, kindly.* Shocked at hearing her voice, I stumbled a bit over my words, but finally said I was looking for availability on particular dates. She tapped at the computer and *after a long inhale through her nose, asked in a clipped voice —*

"Will this be for one or two?"

"Two."

Exhaling through her nose, that is in a quiet snort of disapproval, "Will you want **one** king-sized bed or **two** queens?"

A Light Shining in a Dark Place — 51

"Whatever is available will be fine."

After clicking around the screen, she then said, "What *na-a-a-ame* will this be booked under?" I gave her mine, along with credit card info, and the room was officially booked. I said thank you. Then she *coldly spat out,* "May I ask: Am I speaking to my daughter?"

"If you are [Her Name Here], then yes, you are speaking to your daughter."

Slight pause then a *harsh little laugh that said I knew you were a whore all along,* "Ah. I see." And she hung up.

I had the phone on speaker so my granddaughter could hear me making the reservation. We were having big fun, excited about the adventure. But after Mother hung up, my teenage granddaughter looked at me, eyes wide with shock. She said, "That was Grandma [Name Here]?" I nodded and she blurted, "Oh. My. God. She thinks you're bringing a man!"

Granddaughter was more correct than she knew. Then she started laughing and I started laughing and we went and Mother wasn't working while we were there and she had not told anyone her daughter was coming and I didn't have to worry about anything, so yay for me.

One thing is guaranteed: Mother probably does not remember that at all.

Memory is an interesting thing. While I remember experiences and specific events inside the family and can put these in an autobiographical form (times, places, and other information that gave the memory context), my knowledge about what happened outside the family was limited.

For instance, I was six years old, sitting on the floor almost under the ironing board. Mother was ironing. The TV was on. We were watching when suddenly Mother burst into tears and screamed "No! No! No!"

She was inconsolable. Her crying and screaming were not unknown in my experience. I thought when she reacted like that, that it was something only happening within the family and did not conflate it with anything else. It wasn't until I was an adult with children that I realized Mother was crying and screaming because John F. Kennedy had just been assassinated.

My episodic recall was highly accurate and served as the family's memory. For instance, I reminded them of consequences if chores weren't done. They did not remember the chores or the penalties — and were always surprised when punishments occurred.

It was I who remembered that when Devil held his hands like *this, that* bad thing would happen. Seeing that in time could mean a heads-up to Mother and siblings, hopefully sparing them a beating or other torture. It was I who cataloged the emotions of each person. If I arrived late, that is, after the family had missed all his cues and crap was hitting the fan, it was up to me to read the scene, putting two and three together to get five, and come up with a way to stop it… or at least soften the outcome.

To say that the family's episodic memory was almost non-existent is not off-beam. On the other hand, their semantic memory was awesome. They knew what was happening in the outside world. Drugs, sex, rock 'n' roll, wars, social movements, and popular culture were unknown subjects to me except where they influenced the family. I had not heard about a certain war until the day it was ending …and only found out about it when seeing the entire family huddled around the TV, horrified, shocked, crying, and wringing their hands while watching the last dramatic evacuations on that helicopter. What the heck is going on? Years later that same footage was shown in a documentary. I blurted out, "Wow. That was the Vietnam War?"

Sometimes these lapses in my understanding were comedic. Baby Brother used to call Little Sister Double Dildo. Other than Mother who went "Oh!" and hid her eyes, everybody laughed when our sister went utterly insane. But me? I simply stood there with the equivalent look of "Whuuuut?" I was married a long time before I finally knew what a dildo was and still didn't know what one would do with it. That's when the husband looked at me with "Whuuuut?" And I said, "Well, why do I want this when you've got a perfectly good real one?"

In another example, Mother completely prohibited fourteen-year-old Baby Brother from wearing certain necklaces popular with men at the time. She said only druggie hippies wore them. I was not aware of this ongoing loud conversation and took Baby Brother shopping for clothes. He saw a necklace and asked my opinion of it. Well, I liked it on him and he asked if I would buy it. He seemed very eager to get it. I wanted him to be happy and this would make him happy, so pennies were counted, and it was purchased. He put it on and we got home.

Mother went ballistic and ordered him to take it and the new shirt off.

Baby Brother pointed at me and said I had purchased these for him. Mother wanted to know why the purchase was made against her wishes. I said I had no clue about her opinion on the matter. Mother and Baby Brother stared at me. I had completely missed their discussion about the necklace because it had nothing to do with the safety of the family. It was a disagreement between two people who were not going to try to kill each other. Clearly any noise about that had gone in one ear and out the other and never stuck.

When I was around fifteen, as Mother and Little Sister and I were studying the Bible together, Mother made a comment about how our childhoods were so great and she was so happy about that. Little Sister and I stared at her. She looked back at us and said, "What?"

There is no need to go into the whole conversation here but suffice it to say she was very upset when reminded about how she ordered me to do things to her husband so she wouldn't get beaten and how Little Sister was forced to watch and that, somehow, I did not think that made for a good childhood and, oh by the way, there are more stories about abuse.

Mother burst out crying. Said she did not remember doing those things. She was a good Christian woman and would never. And out of the room she went and we never again studied the Bible together.

As time went on and Mother was widowed, she insisted it was only her that ever was abused by her Honey, my Devil. So, is her memory bad? Is she delusional, mentally ill, or evil? Maybe she can be all. If so, that's a dangerous combination.

Yet many years later she said she apologized to all my siblings for not protecting them when they were children. I have no way of verifying this because I cannot speak to three of my siblings. Little Baby Brother said he remembered she apologized but wasn't quite sure for what. Still, Mother did not apologize to me. Instead, she slowly drove me around her town running her errands as she made excuses saying, "I'm just weak." Of course this I already knew. Was her admission, or confession, to be her agent of change?

Sadly, it did not prove to be and hopes for genuine love from Mother were again dashed.

Trust

Good people believe "trust me" implies that to do so will be good for them. Players of confidence games and other evil people know "trust me" is only going to benefit them and that you — the mark, the victim, the prey, the dupe — will not like what happens once they are gone.

So trust is interesting. One can trust that both good and bad things can happen. While there were few in my life I could trust about good things, there was always that niggling feeling that maybe trust in them was misplaced. In any case, I mostly learned trust was not a good thing.

Yet one cannot go around acting like one suspects everybody of being evil without going nuts. Therefore, I faked trusting. With a smile and a confident handshake, I said I trusted, but if verification was slow in coming, it was time to plan how to get out of or handle the situation. This took a lot of mental energy and kept me in a negative place, both of which kept me drained.

"Trust but verify" took the calmer form of believing the best of everyone until proved wrong. Once they showed their true colors, *BAM!* they were out of my life. This seems to work well —

definitely fit into my need to be the stranger — and has helped with my other problem: How does one share a life with another?

I do not know. I've always been the one that subjugated myself, my wants, needs, and desires for others. It was my job to sacrifice for them. It was my job to be disappointed and smile and move on.

I could take disappointment.

I must not want too badly.

Plans? Why have them when it's my duty to change anything I planned for myself when another's needs must be attended to?

You would think that after 32 years of marriage I would know about sharing, but sharing with one's mate is supposed to be a two-way street with no quid pro quo involved.

That was not my marriage.

But you can rest assured I trusted my husband that he would deliver nothing much good to me. To be fair, I trained him well in doing that.

2010: Open Letter to God

Dear God,

Someone told me that you find me useful. My reply was that you have used donkeys and enemies to deliver your message or otherwise do your will, so that your having used me did not of and by itself prove I was faithful to you or approved by you.

I am trying to do my part by being honest, sincere, and not sweating the small stuff.

I am doing that.

Please, are you doing your part?

I have no doubt that this thing with me will turn out fine…in the long run. And that somehow, somewhere, some way you will find a way to use me to benefit you even in this situation. That has been our path since the beginning.

I am still mad at you, though not as much. I believe you can handle that, yes?

Sincerely,

Angela

Hypervigilance

Take a girl with an inquisitive mind, who likes to plan, doesn't like surprises, and who is Big Helper. Naturally, she is going to walk into any situation and assess the danger and make a plan of action in case A, B, or C presents itself. Then she will look at the crowd, make threat assessments, judge response types among crowd members, identify all points of ingress and egress of a venue she's in, and be quietly so alert that she notices where total strangers are sitting and picks up on all disturbances in the energy of the crowd. Sometimes even walking over to that energy disruptor to disrupt — successfully — the negative energy by bringing in happiness and light and support and understanding and...more things that would take the focus off the negative and onto Angela because, after all, Angela was the Big Martyr Willing To Die For Total Strangers So They Could Be Saved Doncha Know.

And after fulfilling her mission of leaving the disruptor in a positive state, she then goes back to her seat where her husband asks for an explanation and she tells him what he wants to hear even if it is a lie because he really has never understood and he gets all upset and she doesn't want any more negativity around her. And he knows it's a lie she's telling.

And she knows he knows.

But he doesn't have the strength to grant himself the serenity to accept things he cannot change, nor does he have the courage or the will or the want to change the things he can. Most definitely he doesn't have the wisdom to know the difference. Frankly, serenity and wisdom are not in her either, so in this the woman and her husband are a match. Courage and cowardice will be constant themes in her life as a result.

Geez.

I was flat worn out.

Looking to my Heavenly Father, guess what I found? Why, even He allows people to make their own decisions and live with the consequences: He gave us Free Will. So when the realization hit after all these years that I had not yet run into a *Die Hard* or *Black Sunday* situation wherein it was solely I who was responsible for saving absolutely everyone, well then, my ego was shut down.

Yes, prideful ego kept me hypervigilant much longer than I needed to be. Sure, what I did as a child was necessary and I was good at it. Of course there is nothing wrong with planning, being aware of one's surroundings, but when I went into a stadium and had to sit at the highest point with my back against a wall, preferably in a corner where my flanks were protected, and I was having panic attacks after seeing the job was bigger than me but I was the only one...

…blah, blah, blah, boring, and yawn.

I will say it again: I was flat worn out. Nothing good was happening from my behavior. The hypervigilance that took in all information from all points of view only focused on one thing: The negative.

My hypervigilance completely missed all the good stuff. Even alone, every noise had to be investigated and ruled out as having been made by a bad person seeking to do harm to me and mine.

I say again: I was flat worn out.

When I became aware of my hypervigilance, ignoring it became ever more difficult. But with practice, I finally managed to be able to relax more. For instance, if I see two people arguing in public, it is not my job to fix it. I allow them to argue. In fact, I have often watched the argument and studied the people involved to see how they resolved it.

A Light Shining in a Dark Place — 63

One psychologist gave me a tool to use when the emotional response became overwhelming. By touching the clothes I was wearing, feeling the cloth's texture, concentrating on that, I could be brought back into the reality of the situation I was in. It worked great. I've used that touch focus on metal, carpet, leather, paper, ice, and other items, with both hands and bare feet.

The Need to be Remembered

Other than a shared childhood and a weak mother, what else did we siblings have in common? Nothing much. Here was the next ego check, sad to say: Why was it so important to have my family in my life? I could think of but one reason: I wanted acknowledgement of the sacrifices made for them. Heck, I needed it. Was trying to get it.

Then came the understanding that even Jesus Christ, who died for humans and who said no one has greater love than he who lays down his life for another (John 15:13), and his Father, who allowed His son to go through that testing death, do not have their sacrifices acknowledged by the majority of humankind. So who am I to demand that same gratitude from just five people I happened to be related to by blood? Oh, my. That hurt the old ego and I thought: Am I just as sniffingly self-righteous as they? Please, God, if I am, send help to make me see it. And He did. Often. Because, just like Jesus' disciples argued amongst themselves as to who was greatest (Luke 9:46), it took a while for me to check my ego. Yes…still working on it, too.

But then an interesting thing happened. I got to know two cousins: A female on Mother's side I got to know pretty well, the one from California mentioned earlier; and a female on my father's side who lives local to me. In fact, of all my relatives, this one here in Georgia and I are a lot alike. We talk, text, or email just about every day and do projects together around her house. While we're working we're chatting and sometimes arguing, but always enjoying each other's company. And I thought of all the three sisters I've got (Father had two more daughters from a second marriage), Awesome Cousin Number One is more like a sister to me than any other. We are there for each other and isn't that what sisters are for?

So, if I should die before her, I will be remembered for all the right reasons, and so my Heavenly Father has supplied another thing I needed for emotional, psychological, and spiritual growth. Having her in my life has been a positive thing and I thank God for her.

I have grown very close to Little Baby Brother and he to me. Of all the siblings, he and I are a lot alike even though we only have a mother in common. I love him. I do.

Journal Note, November 30, 2010

Three days of gray skies and rain.
Three nights of thunder and crashing.
Weatherman says more's on the way and
All I keep thinking about is what isn't.

It isn't sunny.
It isn't warm.
It isn't calm.
It isn't light.

Thirty years of bad love, no tenderness.
Thirty years of sadness and pretending.
All indications are nothing is gonna change
And all I keep thinking about is what isn't.

It isn't happy.
It isn't loving.
It isn't joyful.
It isn't pleasant.

One year of being in my space all by myself.
Alone every day, sleeping gently at night.
Quiet solitude and peace all around.
And all I keep thinking about is what is.

It is full of friends.
It is full of feeling.
It is full of love.
It is full of hope.

Pretzeling

One way of controlling others was to become what they needed me to be. Acting became second nature until I couldn't tell where I ended and the necessary character began. Someone once told me, "Angela, I never know how you will react. You change constantly." Well, duh. I was hypersensitive to all changes in others and reacted accordingly. Anything to maintain control of the situation so violence would not happen. After all, I was Hypervigilance personified.

I could not recognize myself in pictures nor pick my voice out of a recording. I often wondered who that person was in a reflection when I walked by. I take a lot of pictures of myself since the divorce. I am the selfie queen. But it isn't because I am so in love with my image. It's simply to remind myself what I look like at any given time. I am often surprised at my image…and not always in a good way.

I change constantly and not on purpose. Some days the pictures are very good and sometimes they are very bad. But I keep them anyway. And I'm having fun with my image, even making fun of myself at my own expense, a thing I would never have thought I could do.

Yet the desire to please, control, and so forth is still so strong that upon meeting a man I really like, I immediately pick up on his needs and wants and become that thing. It's an automatic response and I hate it. No longer do I feel confident. I second-guess myself. And the man picks up on that. I even had one man say to me, "Now you are just being disingenuous." He thought I was tricking him because the outgoing, confident woman he met and who so intrigued him had changed 180°, leading him to believe I was playing a game.

I was not lying. I was simply not so good at pretzeling myself into yet another believable shape anymore. Somehow I had sussed out what he needed — but could not be it very well any longer. Which, honestly, was a good thing for me. Sure, I was upset for a bit, but then I thought "To hell with him. If he is unable to live with my imperfections, then he's not the man for me." It was the right call. His comment and my inability meant I was leaving behind these so-called skills, necessary and good for awhile but that had kept me away from the good things God gave to humans.

I was very comfortable in that place…until I wasn't. No one could have been more shocked about that transformation than me. And so the reconstruction of Angela continued.

The problem with hiring an expert is that they already know what they know. So if a company hires an expert that already knows what they know, and what they know has been working for them, but the new company has a system that it is attempting to update and change and improve, then the company has a twofold challenge: Getting rid of the expert's habits and methods and retraining in the new way.

However, experts often take it personally when they are forced to change and next thing you know they are looking for another job.

In essence this is what happened to me. Granted, during my marriage I worked very hard on the negatives ruling my responses and emotions and relationships, which is to say I was imperfect and did not always do well. I was broken.

But given that the marriage was to a man who was also broken yet unwilling to work on himself, I was still stalled in the old ways with no hope of getting out of them without taking drastic action. These old ways were keeping me from bonding with my Heavenly Father. And thus with God's command to "Get out. Get out now!" I was now available for Him to work with me as He chose. How did He choose to teach me?

He sent men to teach me the next thing necessary to work on. Of course, I didn't see a man and say, "Hey, God sent him so he's the one" and jump into a hasty marriage or ill-advised relationship. And while men approached and offered their *services* all the time, there were some men with whom I had completely different experiences. Some lasting a couple of weeks. Some lasting a few minutes. But upon reflecting on that interaction, God's hand in the matter became obvious because with these I learned the next thing to work on.

I always said a prayer after each of the latter interactions, thanking my Heavenly Father for His care, then got busy on the task He set before me. His methods always worked, maybe not timely because I am often oblivious to His hints, pretzeling will always be a natural go-to state because old habits die hard, and both Nature and Nurture are strong in me. But, whereas before it would take me years to recognize what I was doing and even longer to address it, now recognition comes often in an instant and the addressing of it almost as fast.

A Light Shining in a Dark Place — 71

There is a passage in the Holy Bible at 1 Corinthians 9:19-22 that goes:

> *"For, though I am free from all persons, I have made myself the slave to all, that I may gain the most persons. And so to the Jews I became as a Jew, that I might gain Jews; to those under law I became as under law, that I might gain those under law. To those without law I became as without law toward God but under law toward Christ. To the weak I became weak, that I might gain the weak. I have become all things to people of all sorts, that I might by all means save some."*

When I started reading the Bible and came across this scripture, I totally understood how to apply it…at least my fourteen-year-old mind did. See? Even the Apostle Paul was like me! He pretzeled himself, too! And so that reaffirmed in my mind that I was on the correct path to sacrifice myself — my very being, my soul, my character, my identity — so that others would be happy.

Talk about misunderstanding His word. Poor ol' God must've been shaking His head at me. Must've been? He was. It's also easy to imagine some deep sighs on His part.

Suffice it to say, now that I am no longer as worried as I once was about what people think of me, an interesting thing happened. I'm more flexible in how I interact with folks now, doing as Paul did by meeting them where they are.

Still not comfortable being in crowds; they do drain me. But I'm letting them be them and me be me and isn't that a much better thing?

2013: Open Letter to God

Dear God,

I am lonely, God. Knowing you doesn't help. You can't laugh with me. You can't snuggle with me. I am not going to live forever, so what is the point of any of this?

Please, I am begging, give me what I need. I need a loving man. I need him. I. Need. Him.

I must learn to love and receive love or else all is lost and I have nothing.

No worth to anyone and no prospects for the future in any way.

                                                Sincerely,

                                                Angela

The Blue Bracelet

I was in a particularly frantic frame of mind. Had been for awhile — and praying for all the wrong things, I'm sure — when I received an invitation from my daughter to attend a middle school orchestra concert my granddaughter would be playing cello in. (2022: She is in her first year of college now; microbiology, gene research.)

The weather had been rainy for quite some time and I had not had opportunity to clean my car so took time to do it while on my way to their house. After going through the carwash, I pulled around to the vacuum hoses and gave the interior a thorough cleaning, then was on my way.

You need to understand that nobody, absolutely not one person other than me, had been in that car in over two months. I could name everything that was in it, and blindfolded could've put my hand on exactly what I needed. It was always locked, too.

I get to their house, lock the car doors, and go in. We visit for awhile, then granddaughter and I to go my car. I unlock the doors. We get in. Laying between my feet on the driver's side is a bright blue rubber bracelet. I pick it up and hand it to my granddaughter and say, "Oh, this came off your wrist."

She looks at it and says, "That's not mine. I don't have one that color."

Well, where in the heck did that come from? Had I not just completely cleaned the car and it wasn't in there? Had I not driven straight to their house and locked the doors before I went inside? Had I not unlocked the doors to the car before we got in?

Yes. Yes. And yes. So I looked at the bracelet. Printed on it were three words:

Wisdom and Courage.

Immediately I felt a calmness come over me and knew beyond a shadow of a doubt that my Heavenly Father had answered my prayers, but had given me the advice I needed, not what I wanted. I put the bracelet on, vowing to wear it until I no longer needed to be reminded.

The bracelet came off in 2020 because the lesson was learned. Daddy knows his daughter better than she knows herself.

Full Circle

My profile for online dating would read:

Creative. Stubborn. Logical. Helpful. Competitive. Romantic. Practical. A loner needful of adoration. Desirous for justice. Hater of bullies. Loves to cook. Loves to dance. Chuckleheads need not apply. No broke millionaires, please.

Do you think that would get any takers? Yeah, me neither. But of those things listed above, the two that have the greatest overall impact are "desirous for justice" and "helpful". Which is why I was happy to find out that Almighty God had not left humankind on their own. He had a purpose and that purpose, when it went off rail, did not change and He knew immediately what was needed to set it all aright. (Genesis 3:15)

I will not go into all that other than to say true justice will prevail and so I do not get bent out of shape too much when politicians and preachers and other do-gooder activists stir their little pots and beat their little drums and blow their little horns as they pretend to be the saviors of the world's problems that they, only they, understand and can fix.

A Light Shining in a Dark Place — 77

Instead, I will point out that the rest of the list, so much in evidence when I was a child, has now reappeared and thus I am getting back to what God intended me to be all along. He understands delay. He understands when it is time to act.

And so He let me know when it was time to get going and I did. How it came about was this.

My spirit had dried and I could no longer generate real enthusiasm for anything. But there I was, faking a smile, still doing what I had always done, feeling God slipping away faster and faster, but praying, praying, praying for guidance. And He gave it. But I was so entrenched in my own — oh, in what was I entrenched? My own understanding of God, maybe? — so that when His advice came I said definitively that could not be it. So I got smart, see. And I started giving Him the old fleece test. [To read about the original fleece test, see Judges 6:36-40.] If You, Dear Father, want me to do *that*, then make *this* thing happen. If the *other*, then make *that* thing happen.

Oh, I prayed silently, not moving a muscle in my throat and even closing my eyes in case Satan or another demon was watching and would try to fool me with fake answers. In these prayers, it was easy for God to give me the answer I already knew He would approve of. See? I am ever the Big Helper, even to God.

But the answers came back. And not what I expected, either.

I must have misunderstood what He said.

So for the next four years I set about doing more fleece tests. Always the answer was the same and never what I expected it to be. Finally, one summer at a religious convention, surrounded by fifteen thousand fellow worshippers where I again felt as a stranger, I challenged God:

"My dear Father, you know how stubborn I am. You know how dense I can be. You know how I can doubt everything my eyes see and my ears hear when it concerns me. So, listen you, I need you to be more definitive than ever. You. Must. Make. Me. Understand. What. You. Need. Me. To. Do. And you must do it in a way I cannot mistake it. And you must do it right NOW! In Jesus' name I pray. Amen."

And no sooner had those words left my brain than the man on the stage turned toward me and said, "Get out. Get out now."

No one else, even the man who spoke, seemed to notice a thing as he went back to his notes and continued with his lesson.

I immediately bowed my head and prayed in thankfulness. I said, "Oh, You are good."

And upon that is when my journey started to wherever it is God wants me to be. And it has continued apace. Stumbles do happen, but I neither fret nor worry nearly as long nor as intensely as I used to because He has His purpose for me. A purpose I don't know, and may never, yet seems to be working itself out.

2009: Open Letter to God

Dear God,

You created angels because you were lonely. Even you, complete in all ways, perfect with nothing lacking, wanted company. I find this comforting. It means that even more than I could know or ever understand, you understand my mind. We are truly your children.

Of course, by now you know what has happened…and yet I don't think Satan is happy about it. Satan isn't happy because he suspects, probably knows, there is hope for me yet. I have not been broken and I think you still love me.

You know I don't want to feel this unfeelingness. My dear father, still you love me. I think I am feeling this love just a tiny, tiny bit and I like it.

Yet it isn't enough. You know me. You know my heart. You know my mind. I have not betrayed you though others may believe I have. Thank you.

Sincerely,

Angela

Healing and Truth

So the years marched on and I got divorced and I'm praying and I'm working hard to change the shaky parts of my personality and so forth when some family history came my way from a source on Mother's side that shed a brighter light on her. When that information arrived, the question about mental illness was answered. To protect the privacy of the source, who had no idea what it meant, I am not going to mention from whence this information came, but it was impeccable. Again, this knowledge would prove my Heavenly Father sent what I needed when I best needed it.

Within me was the little girl wishing for hugs and approval and smiles from Mama. The more the little girl did not get those, the more she believed she was unlovable. The more she believed she was unlovable, the more she did not know who she was, why she was here, and sought approval from anywhere just to fill those empty places. This did not work out so well in the long run and all my methods weren't working.

Then here came the new information. My mother's complete backstory if you will.

Now I had a broader context upon which to evaluate Mother's actions and attitude toward me and could more accurately deal with my emotions about her. She was definitely mentally ill. I have not attempted to even guess at which type of mental illness (or illnesses?) because, frankly, it doesn't matter. There is no way of verifying my guess and labeling it won't change anything anyway. But I sure did get some peace in my heart, soul, and mind.

I no longer believe Mother is evil. Evil knows what is wrong and does it anyway. Mother tried very hard to be good but her mental — emotional? — weaknesses only allowed for so much flexibility in approaching life. With the new information, I came to realize she does the best she can with what she has.

Of course, the fallout from her choices on me and my siblings was still just as harmful. But the difference between me and Little Baby Brother and the rest of our siblings is that he and I want to hear the truth. We might be afraid of what we will hear, but we both recognize that light shed on dark places can only help. Yes, Little Baby Brother is coming to a better understanding that talking about things does not kill us, only hurts for a short time, and is beneficial in the long run.

Years ago I watched a British movie called *Cold Comfort Farm*. The movie is based on a 1932 comedy novel of the same name. To control her family, the grandmother character manipulates them with a horror only she had seen in her youth. When the family wants to do something she doesn't like, she screws up her face, gets loud and anxious, and says, "I saw something nasty in the woodshed." Invariably everybody backs away and lets her be.

Her grandson, played by Rufus Sewell, was gorgeous. Dumb as a brick, but Lordy did he ever look good on film, which is discovered by an American relative who comes to stay at the farm and next thing you know a Hollywood director is there to sign him up to be In The Movies. Well, that just would not do and Grandma trotted out the famously manipulative line "I saw something nasty in the woodshed."

Everyone froze, as was their habit. Everybody except the Hollywood director who shot back, "Yes, but did it see you?"

At that the grandmother's hold over the family was broken.

I laughed and laughed at that scene and have incorporated those lines into many conversations with myself as a reminder of that hold. You see, Mother and siblings freeze when the specter of accurate memory arises. I say, "Take the power away from these memories by bringing them into the open."

And thus this memoir with the expanded explanation. I grieve for all the energy I've spent for far too long on activity ineffectively employed. But I don't grieve for too long because look what my Heavenly Father has done for me. I would rather honor that which comes from Him than wallow in sorrow brought by humans.

The old children's gospel song written by Harry Dixon Loes says, "This little light of mine, I'm gonna let it shine." He must've read Matthew 5:14-16 where Jesus said:

> *"You are the light of the world. A city cannot be hid when situated upon a mountain. People light a lamp and set it, not under the measuring basket, but upon the lampstand, and it shines upon all those in the house. Likewise let your light shine before men, that they may see your fine works and give glory to your Father who is in the heavens."*

Happy families are a mystery to me. I do not understand them; though I've always attempted to have one, honestly, I've only partially achieved. Preferring the safety of solitude, to this day I get antsy when around a "happy" family for too long. In solitude I don't have to guess at the subtleties or wonder if I trod where angels feared.

In solitude, outcomes don't need to be predicted and wrong results need not terrify. Though I crave it, too much solitude is not a good thing. Proverbs 18:1:

> *"One isolating himself will seek his own selfish longing; against all practical wisdom he will break forth."*

Which brings us to the God-sent healing mentioned before. It came in the form of an aunt on my father's side. I related this in my 2020 book *This Little Light of Mine: Twinkle Revisited* but it bears repeating here.

One year older than my mother, Pearl Naomi Kell Peavy Vonderhaar retired as a full professor and department head with the University System of Georgia. She had a master's degree in English and was beloved by her students. Aunt Pearl was never happier than when she could feed people.

Next-to-youngest of fourteen, she grew up hungry, so food was a big deal, something to be shared when finally gotten, much appreciated when eaten.

She was a well-known and -liked volunteer in several Conyers, Georgia, civic and social organizations. If you wanted something done, Pearl could rattle the bones of lazy volunteers and "gubment types". She was willing to step into the fray and if somebody didn't like her go-get-'em-make-it-happen spirit and attitude, she would say "To hell with them."

She was much loved by her many nieces and nephews who grew up knowing her. She was quietly helpful to countless folks, not tooting her own horn. Widowed at 48, she thoroughly enjoyed over fifteen years of being fancy free, but then marrying a widower when she turned 65. I did not grow up knowing her, but when my husband and children and I moved, we found she didn't live far from us. So Aunt Pearl and I started having lunch and doing things together every now and then. It was her wisdom that kept me sane — and from being stupid — during and after the divorce.

Everywhere we went people thought she was my mother. We looked alike. We were both tall. We both loved making things happen. We talked alike. We had the same sense of humor. We're practical with a thick, stubborn romantic streak running at our very cores.

Her color palette was Summer, mine, Winter; we couldn't share clothes without looking sickly, but oh, how we both loved words. Books were her thing. That she had a writer for a niece simply put her over the moon. She was so happy to say, "This is my niece, Angela **_Kell_** Durden. She's a writer. Lots of published books."

She fairly beamed. A Kell was a writer! I ate it up — while at the same time being uncomfortable with the admiration. Again, something akin to us both. She was one of the trusted relatives who read *Twinkle — a memoir* and was able to fill in many holes for me. Thank goodness she got to see it before her memory went. It was through her and her sister, Aunt Virginia, that I finally got to know my father for the good man that he was. They sent me a series of pictures my father took of himself in a photo booth when he was fifteen.

He twinkled, too. Aha! So that's where I got my twinkle from.

I cried when I saw it.

Pearl never wanted children. She never longed for them like her siblings did. She never missed not having them. Until she was an old woman, that is. Oh, how she loved to see me. Her eyes would light up and I could make her laugh. And she'd tell me some snarky little comment and I would laugh or agree or nod sagely. Aunt Pearl loved my hugs and I loved hers. "What are you working on now?" would be followed by details of this or that project.

Anyway, after seven years of marriage it became very clear Aunt Pearl had Alzheimer's, and her husband, older than she and in worse health and also losing his mind, could not care for her. Adding to the challenges, she had a lifelong menace of insulin-dependent diabetes with a cascading array of other health troubles. She had named me her fallback care person in case her husband was unable. He was unable and I was called upon.

Gladly I took complete control of her life and healthcare with a determination to make the last years she had joyous. No matter how many times I'd say "she's my aunt", staff, nurses, and doctors never failed to ask "How's your mother doing?" I stopped correcting them after a while because, frankly, it felt good to have her as my mother.

I always focused only on the positive with her. She did not like negativity and it badly affected her. In this we were the same, too. One rule for all her visitors was that they had to make her laugh. Tell funny stories of way back when y'all were young and did that thing or went to that place. Pearl had long-term memories and for some time could add details, even correct their stories.

But when her friends started getting weepy, I'd stand behind Pearl and shake a finger at them to stop that, then using gestures would indicate to put on a smile and laugh. Some, so concerned for their loss of a friend, couldn't even for a moment make the sacrifice to pretend to be upbeat. These were hustled out before Pearl had the opportunity to soak in those negative vibes that always had an immediate deleterious affect upon her health.

Even as she lost all memory of everyone and everything, she always knew me. Every day I was at the 24-hour memory care facility, once, sometimes twice. Zealously checking all her meds and questioning and confirming proper care. Keeping the staff on their toes — or else. All hours I'd drop by. If she was in the hospital, so was I, never leaving her side until my cousin would stop by allowing me to go home and shower.

Her bit of fun was going out for lunch or for coffee or riding with me to go check mail at the post office. She adored our outings — until the effort became too much for her. Then it was encouraging her to eat enough. Or exercise a bit more. Or helping to clean up her "accidents". Overseeing her wound care. Tricking her with a happy red plastic shot glass full of pudding laced with Vitamin C and acidophilous while she was on antibiotics. Oh, how she loved that pudding cup delivered by her niece.

Until, finally, hard decisions had to be made and, with her doctor, I stood next to her and explained it was now time to make those hard decisions on her behalf following the very explicit orders she had memorialized in a legal document. Decisions she was happy with. Decisions she knew I would make on her behalf no matter the sacrifice to myself.

Not too long later she was gone and I cried for her and my loss. And so our lives aligned at the right time for us both and, as a result, I no longer miss Mother like I used to and that pain has eased.

God, my wonderful, loving Heavenly Father, knew I needed a mama upon whom I could pour out all my love and attention. He knew Pearl needed a child to adore her. Aunt Virginia said, "I believe God made it so that you would be available for Pearl." Our Father provided for us both. In this I have no doubt.

I do not know what my Heavenly Father has in store for me. I don't know why His eye has been upon me or how He wants to use me. I don't know what paths He will set me upon nor how He will use me to further His will. But this I do know:

He wants me to continue to twinkle.

And so I shall.

1 Corinthians 4:3-5

Apostle Paul

"Now to me it is a very trivial matter that I should be examined by you or by a human tribunal. Even I do not examine myself.

"For I am not conscious of anything against myself. Yet by this I am not proved righteous, but he that examines me is Jehovah.

"Hence do not judge anything before the due time, until the Lord comes, who will both bring the secret things of darkness to light and make the counsels of the hearts manifest, and then each one will have his praise come to him from God."

Praying

There was a so-called fact going around for quite some time. It went like this:

> God made us with four fingers and one thumb on each hand. He did that for a reason. You see, take away any one of the digits on a hand and we lose our grip on what we are trying to hold. See? Of course you do. Tis the same with praying. If you are praying less than five times per day, then you will lose your grip on God.

Not sure how that got started or which well-meaning soul started it. Nevertheless, it was a guilt trip disguised as one point on the ever-helpful list of How To Get and Stay Close To God.

Somebody equated two things as if they were the same, thus explaining God's wisdom of putting five digits on a hand for maximum gripping power simply must equal the minimum daily quantity we should pray every day or else we can't remain faithful.

A Light Shining in a Dark Place — 95

But define faith?

Faith is a form of Object Permanence, a fundamental concept about understanding that something continues to exist even when it cannot be seen, heard, or otherwise sensed. While scientists have not come to a consensus on when that emerges in human development, the Apostle Paul defines faith for us in Hebrews 11:1:

> *"Faith is the assured expectation of things hoped for, the evident demonstration of realities though not beheld."*

Like a lot of people, though, I could easily remember the prayer-quantity analogy and tried to meet its goals without much more thought than that, never questioning. Only, that dictum always felt wrong. It felt fake. It felt like a man-made rule. Where was the Biblical principle behind it? Where in the Bible did it say we had to formally pray a certain amount of times per day or else as is implied?

Or else what? God won't love me? God will condemn me forever? *Or else what?*

Romans 12:12 — "persevere in prayer".

1 Thessalonians 5: 17 — "pray constantly".

Luke 18:1 — "always to pray".

2 Thessalonians 3:1 — "carry on prayer".

None of these mention a specific quantity. So, to meet a preconceived notion of prayer by count made me feel as if I was cheating God Himself. Not honoring His intelligence by turning Him into a very simple accountant, a receiver of requests, a seeker of compliments, and a solver of problems. But is not God more than that?

I concluded He was because we humans are made in His image and boy, oh boy, are we not a complicated group? Yes, we are. So why was God made out to be such a simpleton?

Also, when I began to think more deeply on the subject, I learned that before I knew the rule from the helpful list on How To Get and Stay Close To God, my Heavenly Father had already heard me even when I was not formally praying. How do I know this? Again, Paul tells us in Romans 8:26-27:

> *"In like manner the spirit also joins in with help for our weakness; for the problem of what we should pray for as we need to we do not know, but the spirit itself pleads for us with groanings that cannot be uttered. Yet He who*

searches the hearts knows what the meaning of the spirit is, because it is pleading in accord with God for holy ones."

Almighty God, my Heavenly Father, had His eye on me from my childhood. When I had no understanding of His opposite: Evil. Did not know about Him. Had no words to express the hatred of Evil and its injustices but in my heart railed against it anyway, God knew where my heart was. He knew what I needed.

Living in the moment, I did not understand any of that. But once I slowed down and looked back at my life, I could see it as plain as day. Therefore, I began to look at all the things governing my decision-making process in this light: Was the decision supported by a Biblical principle or a man-made rule or narrow-minded self-interest?

That examination was an interesting process. I won't go into mine here because it will be different for every person. But the upshot was this:

I got many surprises and learned a lot.

And I dared not speak of what I was coming to understand because too many around were more comfortable building their lives around rules than being responsible for their own actions. In other words, they believed doing ABC would guarantee

XYZ. They didn't have to think or feel. It is easy to be a "person of faith" when all one has to do is put a checkmark by a Big Gotta-Do on a list of How To Get and Stay Close To God.

No wonder I was getting further away from Him! The harder I tried to follow rules and the more closely I did follow that ever-helpful list, the further I got away from Him. That is why He knew what I needed and told me to leave my constricting, obstructive environment. Not that it was bad. It just wasn't right for me.

Even when I did that, though, people said, "Angela, you are leaving the protective confines of the fence God has provided to keep you safe."

My response was that a fence could or could not be protective. Concentration camps and jails have fences. The latter protects those outside the fence. The former is for the purpose of destroying those inside it. Also, for the indecision and the spinning of wheels, it is the sitting on the metaphorical fence that nobody likes. And frankly, I had been sitting on that fence my whole life. Some call that being a mugwump. Your mug is one one side of the fence and your "wump" on the other.

It was an uncomfortable place to be, but was familiar and I knew it well. I stayed there for a very good reason: To sacrifice my well-being — and self — for the well-being and comfort of others, there was no thinking involved. Because my motives were good, I did not see that I was also ignoring the advice of God when in Leviticus 19:18 he told the Jews, "…love your fellow as yourself". Jesus quoted it to the young rich man who was looking for Jesus to stroke his ego. Paul and Jesus' brother, James, quoted it in their letters. (Matthew 5:43,44; 19:19; 22:39; Romans 13:9; Galatians 5:14; James 2:8)

I did not love myself, so how could I love my fellow man? I could not. Even Jesus wasn't a martyr every day about everything. He rested. He ate. He went to parties. He provided wine.

I had done a fine job of training all around me to expect that I was available to help them not just with their burdens but also with their daily loads. (Galatians 6:4,5) So when I began questioning why I was doing that and attempting to learn to love myself, it threw a lot of people for a loop.

Still, I felt less hypocritical praying out loud for others, as in a group before a meal or at a sickbed, than I was praying individually and silently for myself. But I kept on with the guilt trip: Angela, are you praying at least five times each day? The answer was always no.

But I was groaning that which I could not put into words and those groanings unuttered had worked when I didn't know Him. They had worked when I tried to know Him but was stumbling around. So I listened to Him when He made it perfectly clear I was to shut up and wait. (Romans 8:26) So shut up and wait I did.

And you know what?

It worked very well indeed. Not fast. Certainly slower than I wanted it to. But each day I find myself getting closer to my Heavenly Father, my daddy, than ever before. I feel like the teenager who thinks his father is stupid, doesn't care, and hasn't got a clue, but forty years on can see how wise Dad had been all that time.

I like that feeling. It is part of a childhood I never had. Somebody once told me that all humans experience the same things, just not in the same order or in the same depth. My friend was right. I'm living my life in reverse. I went from being the one in the room with all the answers for the out-of-control adults seeking her wise advice, she by necessity having to control them and getting the big head in return, to experiencing the comfort and joy and safety a child feels when they are in the arms of a loving parent.

I enjoy that.

So, how has all this shaped my prayers and, even more importantly, my spiritual path? Let me tell you one story that will help explain it.

After my divorce was final, I bought a small fixer-upper 1/1 condo. As I am a writer and work from home, I made the bedroom into my office and began looking for a wall bed to install in the living room. I found one and hired a company to install it two weeks before the end of 2010.

A few months previous to that, a friend said, "Angela, you need to go out dancing." Mary, a fellow author and a professor and researcher, introduced me to what is known as social dancing. You don't need a date. You just show up and folks dance together. Men can ask women. Women can ask men. If all you want to do is dance, then that's all that would happen.

Going dancing helped me learn what I had missed about human nature but needed to know.

As a child my ego had been built up in a wrong way. (I was the all-powerful wise child who could save the world.) As an adult, I had allowed my husband to systematically destroy any ego I had. (I could do nothing right or well, all other women were better than me and, by the way, he was doing me a favor by allowing me to live in his house.)

Suffice it to say, my ego, my self-esteem, was a deep, empty well of need.

However, besides God, Satan was keeping an eye on me, too. What Satan saw was that I liked male attention…and I needed male attention. Going out to dance in social situations was bringing me a lot of what I needed. Satan assumed I was exactly like my mother who from the age of thirteen had been having sex with many boys and men because she had the craving.

So, a few days before the end of the year in 2010, just about three days after the wall bed install, I was out dancing. A particular man showed up whom I had never before seen. This was not unusual. He was a fabulous dancer and paid me a lot of attention and I liked it. All that evening he kept rotating back to me until by the end of the evening, with folks going on home, we were almost alone. Wow, he was such a good dancer, I can't even begin to explain. And funny and witty on top of that. I had a great time.

The DJ called "Last dance!" and the man and I finished up the evening. After that dance was over, I held out my hand to shake his and say thank you. He said, "Well?" I said, "Well… what?" He said, "What are we gonna do now?"

A Light Shining in a Dark Place

"I'm going home to sleep. I do not know what you are going to do."

"You mean, I'm not coming with you?" he said angrily, thus not a happy camper.

"Noooo," said I.

His eyes went dark and he said, "Bitch! I've wasted all evening on you." He turned and stomped off.

I laughed, thought it was funny, and headed home. I get into bed about one in the morning and fall fast asleep.

Suddenly someone is yelling, "Get up! Get up NOW!" and I jump straight out of bed and whip around looking for the person. I see no one. Heart racing, adrenaline pumping, I wonder what happened. Nobody is outside, either. I try to get back in the bed but cannot.

I go in the kitchen and get something to drink. Come back out and attempt to get in the bed again. But no matter what I do, I cannot get past the edge of the bed and back in. Flummoxed, I look around to think this through. Fifteen minutes I've been trying to get back in the bed and cannot. What is going on? I look up at the ceiling light and say, "Huh. That's weird." Then BOOM!

The heavy steel, wall bed frame crashes to the floor, ripping out the attached shelving unit and huge chunks of wall with it. Had I gotten in that bed I would have been trapped. For sure smothered if not crushed. Nobody would've heard me hollering. After not hearing from me, my children would've found my body and it would not have been pleasant. And BOOM! Just like that I knew it was Satan, or one of his demons, who tried to kill me because he was so mad I had not taken that man home.

Just like that I knew Satan and his demons had no correct understanding of me.

And also *BOOM!* Just like that I knew an angel from God had been watching to protect me. And protect me he did when he screamed into my conscious mind, "Get up NOW!"

I began crying and praying out loud, thanking God for protecting me against Satan's evil scheme. This was the beginning of my understanding of prayer. It is communication. No one communicates with everybody in exactly the same way. Why does the belief persist that we can only approach our Heavenly Father in such strict and formulaic ways or only on a particular schedule? "God is greater than our hearts and knows all things," the Apostle John tells us in 1 John 3:20.

Through the years, I've told this story to a few people. Responses vary from "I don't believe it. I think it was just you being aware even in your sleep" to "There is no God. There is no Satan. You are deceiving yourself."

I stand my ground in reply. "Believe what you will, but I was there and I know what happened. I will not — nay, I cannot! — deny what I know to be true of Him."

In each case, their reply is, "Well, if you are that sure, then it would be wrong to deny your own experience."

In this they are correct. And that is what this book is about: My own experience with my Heavenly Father. I make no apologies for any of it and do not regret including all I do. As mentioned at the beginning: Your experience may differ.

But it isn't any less of an experience with God than mine is. Discovery of a path and walking it are two parts of the same journey.

Psalm 40:12

"For calamities encircled me until there was no numbering of them. More errors of mine overtook me than I was able to see; They became more numerous than the hairs of my head, and my own heart left me."

Putting it Together

Connecting with humans is not easy for me. Sure, I can fake it like nobody's business, but when someone is out of my life, I don't miss them. In fact, I rarely think of them. Often they cease to exist in my mind. Memories of them are carefully sealed and stored.

Yet their opinions, such as "Angela, you are one cold bitch" and "Angela, you are the warmest person I've ever met", play havoc with my mind. Which is true? As a walking, talking dichotomy, deducing the truth about myself has proved challenging. Yet those two opinions are as far from each other as the poles on the earth and never the twain shall meet. For years, lurching from one outside opinion about myself to another, I never once saw my Heavenly Father's opinion of me unless it was filtered through the eyes of a human.

But what was His opinion alone? As of this writing I have been unable to describe it and that searching journey is what this book is all about.

I mentioned earlier about my mother's craving for male attention and that to get it she slept with any male who asked. The hard fact is that I am more like Mother than I want to admit but with one big difference: I don't have sex with every man who asks. Which is not to say that saying no is easy. Like I am loath to say but is true: I admit I'm like my mother in that need. So the craving is there, but not the same actions as she during my childhood or later.

When Mother was about forty-two, a few years after being widowed from her abusive husband and my stepfather, she went out on a date. As she always did when I was a kid, she told me all about it. They had a great time. He was a nice man. He walked her to her door. But then he went over the line: He kissed her. She slapped him. Said he was an immoral man and never to call her again. She slammed the door in his face.

"Mom! All he did was kiss you goodnight. Why did you do that to him?"

"Because I know what he wanted," she sniffed righteously in reply.

"Yes, but Mom…all men want that. That doesn't make them immoral for wanting what God rightly gave us to feel the need for."

"Well, I am never going to deal with any men again." And that was that. At the time of that conversation I had masterfully hidden those same inclinations in myself.

As of this writing my mother is over eighty years old and has never once ever again entertained the idea of having a man in her life because she can't imagine there being any good ones. Or is it that she does not know how to control her response enough to test out the man's proper intentions? That makes me sad. To have lived this long and not realized there are good men cannot be what God had in mind.

Then I met a man who caught my eye in a way no other had. He thought I was just the cutest, smartest, hottest thing ever. Other men think that too, and they make their requests known in a way that does not allow for a relationship. They just want to boink me and when I wouldn't, they'd just leave me be. This other fellow, though, did not act like that. In fact, he was very kind and giving and not selfish. Of course, this totally threw me for a loop because I was not used to that kind of man.

Naturally, I got all bent out of shape because I didn't know what to do with such a fellow. So used to other men's ways, I didn't have to think about how to react with them.

He had been married twice before. Had a high-stress job. Other things he had to take care of with aging parents and sick relatives. I had not too recently come off of looking after my Aunt Pearl for quite some time, plus had other things going on that needed my attention. So, here we were, both with issues we must deal with. Both liking each other a lot but neither wanting to marry again so soon nor live together. Both not wanting to disappoint but needing to handle the lives we were given.

Expectation postponed was making my heart sick. This went on for about eighteen months. Almost three weeks passed during which we did not see or talk to each other, then he came over and we watched a movie. He is a tactile man. He likes to hold hands, caress my hair, and kiss. I liked the same. But on this night I was jumpier than a cat on a hot tin roof.

Every time he touched me, I flinched, jumped, jerked, and otherwise was going nuts. I kept stopping the movie and talking about the plot, dialogue, and action. I got up and used my inversion stool to stretch my back and watched the movie upside down for a bit.

He could tell something was up but didn't ask. He just quietly said nothing. When the movie ended, I said, "Well, see you later" and shoved him out the door with a bye-bye wave and a firm slam.

I am always amazed at how my Heavenly Father provides just what I need when I need it.

During those three weeks of want and need and expectation postponed, I did the unthinkable: I responded just like Mother did on that long-ago date night. I reconciled myself to never needing the touch of a man ever again. I was good with that. "See?" I told myself, "I don't need a man." What I was really saying was that I didn't need the ego blow of him not needing me.

I did such a good job of reconciling myself to it that when the touch of a man did happen, I overreacted. Each time he touched me it was an electric shock to my body, a body that had taken the mind's clue that touch of any sort would never happen again. But I didn't yet know that was what I had done until he showed up. When he left I sighed audibly, relieved he was gone, even hoping I would never hear from him again. During the night I woke with a start. Holy cow. Did I really want to be just like my mother? The answer: Absolutely not.

A few days later I invited the man back. I said, "I'm cooking. You've got to eat." He liked my cooking, so it wasn't difficult to get him over. I fed him, then he turned his chair toward me and I turned mine toward him. Plunking my legs up into his lap, I sat up straight and put my hands together and said, "I need to tell you something that will affect us both."

I could tell from his reaction — he got very still and attempted a noncommittal "I'm listening" expression — that he thought he was getting the final boot and that the meal I had served was his last from me.

Practicing for at least two days as to how I would explain this, when I saw his expression my approach changed. Snap! While this was all about me-me-me, he-he-he was affected, too, so I couldn't just stomp all over the explanation willy-nilly. I got quiet and came at it from a different direction and — though I felt like it, I was determined not to get weepy — so began.

Explaining I was more like Mother than I ever wanted to be, I was determined to learn a new and better pattern of communication. That practice would start with him. I won't go into it all here because it was specific to us.

I told him God sent him because He knew what I needed to move forward in my spiritual path, a path on which my spinning wheels sometimes got bogged down even as I reminded myself what another friend told me: God is not a race.

Just that quickly, my angst went away. But how would the man take it? Honestly, I was no longer hanging my entire future on his decision. He would want to stick around or he wouldn't. Either way, my spiritual wheels would no longer spin in a mire of muddled decision-making process.

But the man understood. And he thanked me for allowing him to be a part of my process and for being frank and open with him about it. Truthfully, my process was changing his process, too. He said he was not going anywhere. In that simple statement he let me know I was valuable to him. Time would tell what that really meant to him.

This conversation with this particular man was part of my journey and was summed up by a social media friend who posted this:

I am definitely responsible for what I say.
I am not responsible for how you interpret it.

This was a big lesson. Part of my normal learned response to the world was to control how the world reacted in order to save others, often from themselves. Isn't this what I'd been doing with Mother and siblings all those years? Had not saving myself always been last? But on this day I was learning it was not a bad thing to put myself, my needs, first and let someone care for me if they so chose to do it.

I was learning that I could let someone care for me without sacrificing myself by pretending to be weaker than I was.

I was learning to share my emotional, psychological, and spiritual burdens but carry my own load at the same time.

I was learning that I could look after myself and not exclude others from my life.

I was learning that I could put myself first yet still care for the other person's needs but in a way that left them dignity.

I was learning I could show my flaws and in that showing the path to my Heavenly Father became clearer, more open, less obstructed by ego and pride.

For quite some years Mother had kept on at me about leaving my husband. She kept saying he was not good, not nice, bad even. "Move in with me. Bring the children. You don't need a man," she said more times than I could count.

A day came when my husband and I went over to her house to repair something outside. We paid for it out of our meager funds. He did all the work with my youngest brother, still living at home with Mother, there as his gofer. I was inside with her and there she started again to get me to leave him.

I got tired of it and snapped, "You're just jealous I found a good man and you never did."

Whoa. That was not the right thing to say and off she went on me in a quietly self-righteous way as she explained how it was only her that got hurt by her husband and she didn't know why I was complaining about my childhood. Much more was said that day, most of which I have forgotten, but it led to things I have not forgotten to this day.

Drawing herself up straight and tall, lifting her nose in the air and looking at me down the length of it, she sniffed loudly and announced, "I am proud of my humility."

That stopped me dead in my tracks. Husband was finished with the project by this time and we left. But from outside, hubby and brother heard our raised voices. Husband asked about it. Of course I told him what she'd been trying to get me to do all those years.

Still, what she said stuck. How can one be humble (or, as Mother always said it, 'umble) and be proud of it at the same time?

This was my next lesson. I had some of the same prideful traits in me that she did, and boy oh boy did that ever hurt my feelings. Thankfully, these were tempered by Nature from Father's side of the family and my own Free Will. So, while

Mother could not change nor even see she needed to, my father's DNA meant I was capable of questioning myself and not only seeing what needed changing but with Free Will be willing to work on it.

I was very grateful for that.

But with this fellow I was having to think. And for the next six months think I did until finally realizing his good qualities had been exaggerated to the exclusion of the negative ones. And that is what has been another of my superpowers: Inflating and conflating and deflating reality. For instance —

He was very kind and helpful — but only when it suited his schedule.

He was giving — but it was talk only, no follow-up action on promises made.

He was selfish — everything all about him.

In other words, I had picked somebody just like myself. Had I simply traded one apex of the swing of my emotional and psychological pendulum for its opposite?

Was I excusing these in myself while holding him to a higher standard of care? And was I really learning all those lessons outlined a few pages back? Here's what happened with that man and what I realized about myself.

After two years of politely being ignored by him (remember, only when it suited him did he seek my company), he took a two-week driving vacation to where he was born and raised, visiting family on his way out and back.

This was not to be an easy trip as either bridges would be burned or crossed. Before he left I had a moment of clarity about the future: He is going to move west when retiring. Did I want to move with him? Would he want me to move with him? [How this man was acting was not wrong, but his life wasn't a fit for me.]

During his two weeks gone I did a lot of thinking, soul searching if you will, and realized a few things.

One: For the first time in my life I had built a life I could call my own and I liked it. So, if I did not want to marry him and share his life, what is the point of continuing to build the relationship?

Two: For the first time, I found I would *miss* people — including my children — and a cousin and some creatives in the music world, as well as my editor, and some others.

Three: I'd worked hard establishing myself in the book and music scenes. People knew me.

Four: I did not want to be a stranger again and if I moved and lived out in the desert with this man in solitude and quiet, I would again be burying myself, sacrificing to the needs of another who would, as time went on, be merely tolerating my presence because he needed to be alone. But the big ones were five and six.

Five: I did not want to be in a relationship ever again if it meant I had to share my physical space, watching out for when I made noise (as I am often up in the middle of the night writing) so as not to disturb his sleep. Also, I came to the realization that my role as Big Helper — set in DNA and identified by Mother when I was fifteen months old — would always be fighting to be the most important thing.

That's when another aha! moment happened. Just like Mother gave up men, I too decided to give up men. Both of us for fear of doing something wrong against God. She, morally. Me by ignoring where He wanted me to be that worked best for both Him and me. He'd certainly been working very hard at it and I thought it best not to ignore Him any longer.

And six: If a man ever were to be in my life again, he would have to fit into my life first, foremost, and always.

When the man came back from his trip, I told him we needed to have a chat and we met at a restaurant. While we ate, he told me of his travels and so forth. But his facial expressions were unlike his normal pattern, and his body language was completely set for incoming bad news. As we finished eating, I said, "Well, I've got to say a few things about us."

And so he was informed that we were not a match, and I did not want to leave the life I had built to go live in the desert with him and have to start all over. Further, if he was being honest with himself, he didn't want to live in the desert with anyone either, no matter how cute and smart and fun and awesome. And therefore, from this moment on, he and I would not be seeing each other again.

Clearly he was of two minds on this.

One: Crap!

Two: YAY!

I smiled. He smiled. But over the course of about a minute or so, the smiles changed to reflect upon our new reality. They went from Okay to Oh to Right.

We took one last walk together. He stood, not knowing what to do. I put him out of his misery with a goodbye hug and a consoling pat, got in my vehicle, and drove away not looking back.

So there. Definitive. No more dating because I am no longer looking. Sure, if I go out dancing, I'll dance with a man and say "Thank you kindly, sir" and walk away. If God wants me married, then He will simply have to supply the man in such an overt way that this daughter of His cannot be tricked.

I laughed when I read what I just wrote above because, as we all know, when Angela plans, God laughs sympathetically — and not unkindly.

Which is not to say I do not long for a man on various levels. During the middle of the night, when the longing is sharp, rethinks are only natural. But when the light of day dawns, the will is stronger and the resolve renewed.

Afterword

If you've made it here then you've probably seen one thing clearly: I still don't have my life figured out.

But what I have figured out is that change is constant. Being flexible with where God wants me to be and doing what He needs me to do saves time and trouble in moving along productively in the life He has for me to live — whether or not I am comfortable with it.

Another thing that's important is that He provides the best way for individuals to learn. In reviewing my life I saw several very specific times He sent lessons. As I became better at identifying those lessons more quickly, the faster I learned and the more my angst decreased.

I've also come to understand that rules based on human understanding of His word can often be wrong and that the codifying of those into hard and fast directives as if they come from God Himself limits God's love and care from coming through in a timely fashion.

Being a person who is most comfortable with the black and white of the decision-making process, learning to accept the grays of my Heavenly

Father's dealings with mankind has been tough. Long-ingrained habits of thinking and reacting are hard to break; therefore, diligence in paying attention to those when they rise is of prime importance in continuing to move forward in a productive fashion. The grays may be hard to live in, but they are much more fascinating and fulfilling.

One thing has become increasingly clear. Proverbs 22:6 says: "Train up a boy according to the way for him; even when he grows old he will not turn aside from it." This is often quoted to remind Christian parents of their commitment to teaching their children about God and life and so forth.

But as I've gotten to an age where I am far away from my childhood, I find those lessons I was taught and those ways of thinking and reacting I was trained in are still strong. The struggle not to give in to Satan and his cronies and to keep up the battle against them is lifelong. Has it been worth it? Yes. Have I tired out and wanted to give in and just not worry about God anymore? Yes. When I think God is no longer aware of me, I remember the prophet's words in Isaiah 40:27-31, in part here:

"He is giving to the tired one power; and to the one without dynamic energy he makes full might abound. Boys will tire out…and young men…will stumble, but those hoping in Jehovah will regain power. They will mount up with wings like eagles. They will run and not grow weary; they will walk and not tire out."

This is the promise upon which I rely.

After-Afterword

For all intents and purposes, this book was finished. Had I not definitely stated in **Sibling Update** that I had fully accepted my family's limitations toward me? Well, funny how things show up and connect. Two events occurred which I shall briefly relate to you here.

In late 2020 I was hired by a couple to oversee a book project on the subject of moving through grief after the death from a long-term illness of a loving and much-loved spouse. I've never had such an experience, but got busy on the subject and within a year the book was almost ready for publication.

July 5, 2021: I get the news that Baby Brother (who lives in New York) was just getting out of ICU. When I asked Little Baby Brother in Georgia why our brother had been in ICU, he replied, "Oh, crap. I forgot to call and tell you that. I'm so sorry. What happened was he tripped and fell while holding a nail gun and a big ol' nail went into his head."

He sent me the picture of the nail in Baby Brother's temple taken by his daughter, who had found her father (having just turned 60 on July 3) stumbling around the house.

She asked, "Daddy, do you know you have a nail in your head?"

The story Baby Brother told his daughter, doctors, and his wife was that he tripped and accidentally shot himself in the head with this big, heavy nail gun. I hung up and promptly fell to crying for all the reasons you can imagine.

Baby Brother and I had been estranged for 20 years or so. He had told me never to call him again and I had honored his wish all these years, but that didn't stop me from remembering how he had been in a psych ward for about three months on suicide watch not long after his second marriage — or so said our mother, who called me horribly upset about possibly losing her son. But as was normal in our family, Angela was not to broach those subjects and so I didn't all those years until now, when I told Georgia brother, who had never heard that.

In any case, I cried for Baby Brother almost two days straight with worry about what was driving him to suicide and blew up Little Baby Brother's phone with texts and calls to try to get updates on his condition. Little Baby Brother eventually got hold of Baby Brother and my phone finally rang.

"Good news, Angie. Just got off the phone and [NY brother] explained it all and sure enough shooting himself in the head with the nail gun was a total accident so that other thing you were thinking just isn't so. And I told him you were blowing up my phone in worry about him and he said OK and didn't sound mad or mean or anything and so I think you should call him. I think you oughta and I think it will be alright, especially if you just ask how he is. Be light and breezy and encouraging like you know how to do."

It took parts of two days before I got the courage to call. I will spare you the details, but let it be sufficient to say that Georgia brother's assessment of NY brother's changed opinion of me was way off base. Baby Brother hung up on me before I could even ask how he was. Technology being what it is, I thought the abrupt end to the call may have been weather-related and called back only to have his wife answer. He couldn't come to the phone and they were in the mountains, sooo…. I asked that when they got home if he could return my call that would be awesome. Silence then, not warmly, a reply, "I'll pass along the message."

Alrighty then.

The next day, though, came a text from his phone that was definitive: Baby Brother wanted nothing to do with me because of three reasons. One, I had been shunned by our religion. Two, if I hadn't been shunned I was certainly living a life that required shunning. And three, even if one and two were not true, then he was very unhappy with how I'd been treating our mother in the last few years, and so if he got word that Mother and I had "made up" then he would resume our relationship.

Well, seeing as how in the last few years Mother would not even answer the phone when I called, I had certainly not written her any letter, and when visiting Little Baby Brother who said he'd go with me to visit her, she had said she was very busy and didn't have the time for us to drop by. In any case, confused as to what my sins against her were, I thought —

Okay.

Whatever.

Wished for and granted.

I can take a hint.

Little Baby Brother wanted to know how the call turned out. I told him and he said, "Well, guess you got your answer. I tell ya, if somebody don't want me, then I don't want them either."

July 19, 2021: I had a meeting with the client mentioned earlier and realized that God had put us together for two different reasons and we had a long conversation about what those were. For my part, I believed it was because my Heavenly Father was teaching me what a happy couple could actually look like so I could be more open to the possibility of a future mate after loss.

Later that evening I met with a friend for coffee and a chat whereupon we talked of recent developments with NY brother (this friend had already read this book and was familiar with my journey). Like a car going the wrong way on a crowded interstate, an epiphany hit me, as epiphanies are wont to do.

In other words, I couldn't miss it.

The main lesson God wanted me to learn from this couple was not about love, but about grief: The free expression of it, the willingness to experience it, the not denying that it exists.

Grief was not something to be feared.

You see, I told my friend, I've denied that I missed the brother and mother and sister, all of whom wanted nothing to do with me. I often thought that when they died you wouldn't find me crying. Oh, no. I'd be smiling and moving on with my life, not telling anyone about the loss because there had been no loss and hadn't it been they who pushed me away?

So what was there to miss?

But my friend said, "Angela, you won't be missing him so much as you will miss the having of a brother. And you're feeling the same way about your mother."

And she was right. It mightn't be Baby Brother himself or Mother or Little Sister I'd grieve for when they were gone, but I'd be grieving for the missed opportunity for those loving relationships.

And so my friend and I, sitting in a Dunkin' Donuts sharing a small bag of Munchkins and sipping coffee, talked of grief and grieving and God's wonderful timing in providing the right people to help understand grief and the time to sit with the knowledge because He knew what was going to be needed.

Earlier that day I had looked at my clients and said, "God truly is good." They nodded in agreement. Later that early evening, the expression on my friend's face said the same thing to me. As I write this, I nod in agreement.

One last insight should bring a smile: While I have determined that I will probably not marry again, and am quite comfortable and happy living alone, I was telling my friend about the Bluegrass Jam I had been attending at a live music venue in Atlanta on some Thursday nights. I was able to sing with these guys and had even been invited to stay up on stage and harmonize with them after I sang my original song. They were my kind of men. I said to my friend, "You know what I have just realized. If I ever do get a man, it should be a cowboy. I need a cowboy."

She laughed loudly. I laughed loudly and slapped my knee in major mirth. The Dunkin' staff stared at we crazy women.

Other Scriptures the Author has found extremely helpful

- 2 Chronicles 33 — Learning the hard way.
- Titus 1:15 — All things are clean to clean people.
- Romans 14:14 — Nothing is defiled in itself; only where one thinks it is, it is.
- Isaiah 53:6 — We have all wandered, turned to our own way; Jah causes our error to meet up with him.
- 1 John 2:1 — We have a helper if we sin.
- John 16:33 — In the world we have tribulation.
- Micah 7:18 — God pardons error and passes over transgressions. He delights in loving-kindness and does not hold onto anger.
- Psalm 119:176 — Have wandered, lost. Look for me. I have not forgotten you.
- Ecclesiastes —

    3:1-8 — There is a time for birth and death, planting and uprooting, etc.

    4:2, 3 — Better to be dead than alive, but better still never to have been.

4:9, 10 — Two are better than one. A partner can raise you up.

7:7 — Oppression can make the wise one act crazy.

7:8 — Better is the end of a matter than the beginning.

7:20 — There is not one righteous man who does not sin.

TWO SONGS THE AUTHOR WROTE that you may enjoy attempting to play on a guitar or piano.

CAN YOU HEAR ME, DADDY?
12-BAR BLUES Bm F#m Em
Chord pattern goes for all verses.
Sung slowly, as in prayer.
Each verse is 12 bars. 4/4 time

VERSE ONE:
Bm (4 bars)
Our enemy has chased me, 'til I
fainted dead away. I
spread out my hands to you, Oh, Daddy,
Can you hear me pray?
Em (2 bars) | Bm (2 bars)
Daddy?   Oh, Daddy,
F#-   E-   B-   B-
(One bar each chord change)
Can you   hear me   pray? (Music only)

VERSE TWO:
Do not judge me harshly in this
hour of my fall.
I'm not a righteous woman, Oh, Daddy,
Can you hear me call?
Daddy? | Oh, Daddy
Can you   hear me   pray? (Music only)

VERSE THREE:
I am exhausted.
I've reached the end.
Do not hide from me.
Your love, please send, OH!
Daddy? | Oh, Daddy
Can you   hear me   pray? (Music only)

VERSE FOUR:
Will I see the morning?
I thank you for this talk.
Deliver me, oh my daddy,
I need help to walk.
Daddy? | Oh, Daddy
Can you   hear me   pray? (Music only)

VERSE FIVE:
The morning sun is rising,
it's coming o'er the hill.
I love you, Daddy, Oh, Daddy,
Can you hear me still?
Daddy? | Oh, Daddy
Can you   hear me   pray? (Music only)

CAN YOU HEAR ME, DADDY? | © 2016
GOD IS NOT A RACE | © 2017
Used with permissions from
Angela K. Durden and Second Bight Publishing

GOD IS NOT A RACE

Sung slowly, as in prayer.
3/4 time (also known as Waltz Time)
(One chord per measure)

CHORUS 1:
  |C |C |F |F
If I don't believe, Lord, why do I keep praying for
|G |G |F |C |C
help and comfort from someone I can't see? [MUSIC]
  |C |C |F |F
If I am not worthy of your kind a--tention,
|G |G |F |C |C
why do I keep praying on sore, bended knees [MUSIC]

VERSE ONE:
|F |F |F |F
Oh, oh, oh, Oh Lord, [M U S I C]
|Am |Am |Am |Am
I am so   old now. [M U S I C]
|F |F |F |F
[M U S I C] Not many   years   [M U S I C]
|Am |Am |Am |Am
are left to me.   [M U S I C]
|F |F |F |F
Oh, oh, oh, I've been told MUSIC
|Am |Am |Am |Am
by many a saint   MUSIC MUSIC
|Em |Em |Em |Em
that nothing I do   MUSIC
|G |G |G |G
can save my soul. [M U S I C] So…. **[CHORUS ONE]**

A Light Shining in a Dark Place — 137

VERSE TWO:
|F |F |F |F
Oh, oh, oh, Oh Lord, [M U S I C]
|Am   Am |Am |Am
I've been con- demned [M U S I C]
|F |F |F |F
by many who point out [M U S I C]
|Am |Am |Am |Am
my eternal resting place. [M U S I C]
|F |F |F |F
Oh, oh, oh, Oh,   [M U S I C] a
|Am |Am |Am |Am
wise friend just told me [M U S I C]
|Em |Em |Em |Em
He said, "Child…" [M U S I C]
|G |G |G |G
"God is not a race." **[CHORUS TWO]**

CHORUS 2:
|C | C |F |F
You know I believe, Lord, because I keep praying
|G |G |F | C | C |
For help and comfort from someone I can't see? [MUSIC]
|C |C |F |F
I know I'm not worthy of your kind a-ttention, but I
|G |G |F |C
thank you for caring for poor wounded me

ACKNOWLEDGEMENTS

I am forever indebted to Tom Whitfield. His editing never ceases to amaze me. He has the eye of an eagle and the willingness to allow this writer to break rules if it will help her tell her tale. Tom is a true friend…no doubt one sent by my Heavenly Father.

To **Terry Cantwell,** who helped me see that God is not a race.

To the **Jedwinistas**, my writing critique group: Jim, Candis, Cathy, Fred, Ron, Jedwin, and Sean. They got first look at this book; their responses proved to be very helpful.

And to my friend, **Misha**, who himself is reviewing life, with whom I've had many frank conversations, and whose questions and honesty are spot on. Besides, you don't know what fun is until you have a native Russian speaker talking fast in English while he's laughing at the most hilarious joke he just made and of which you have only caught every third word but those are so funny you're laughing anyway and trying not to spew coffee.

Other books by Angela K. Durden

Eloise Forgets How to Laugh (2004) (eBook)

A Mike and His Grandpa Story:
Heroes Need Practice, Too!
(2006, hardback) — www.angeladurden.com
(2012, paperback) — Amazon.com
Available in English, French, and Spanish

A Mike and His Grandpa Story:
The Balloon That Would Not Pop!
(2012) — Amazon.com

Opportunity Meets Motivation:
Lessons From Four Women Who Built
Passion Into Their Lives and Careers
(2010) (out of print)

Men! K.I.S.S. Your Resume and Say Hello to a Better Job (2013, audio book) — iTunes and Audible.com

Men! K.I.S.S. Your Resume and Say Hello to a Better Job
(2013) — Amazon.com

9 Stupid Things People Do to Mess Up Their Resumes (2000)
(out of print)

First Time For Everything (2018)

Do Not Mistake This Smile (2018)

Dancing at the Waffle House (2019)

Music Business Survival Manual (2018)

Navigating the New Music Business as a DIY and Indie
(2015)

Conversations in Hyperreality — and Other Thoughts
Umberto Eco and Dave Barry Never Had
(2019)

Twinkle — a memoir (2015)

This Little Light of Mine: Twinkle Revisited (2020)

Books by Durden Kell

Whitfield, Nebraska
(2015)

Smith and Jones Mystery:
The Case of the Snuff Tape Killers
(2021)

An Adman Mystery:
Death in E minor 9[mm]
(2020)

Death on the Downbeat
(2021)

… A Light Shining in a Dark Place

NOTES YOU MAY WANT TO MAKE:

NOTES YOU MAY WANT TO MAKE:

A Light Shining in a Dark Place — *143*

NOTES YOU MAY WANT TO MAKE:

NOTES YOU MAY WANT TO MAKE:

A Light Shining in a Dark Place — *145*

NOTES YOU MAY WANT TO MAKE:

Blue Room Books Publishing
Decatur, GA
BlueRoomBooks.com

A Light Shining in a Dark Place
ISBN-13: 978-1-950729-14-2

Made in the USA
Middletown, DE
12 March 2022